WITHDRAWN

DARLINGTON
International Raceway
1950–1967

Tom Kirkland & David Thompson

MBI Publishing Company

First published in 1999 by MBI Publishing Company,
729 Prospect Avenue, PO Box 1, Osceola, WI 54020-0001 USA

© David R. Thompson and William T. Kirkland, 1999

All rights reserved. With the exception of quoting brief passages for the purpose of review no part of this publication may be reproduced without prior written permission from the Publisher.

The information in this book is true and complete to the best of our knowledge. All recommendations are made without any guarantee on the part of the author or Publisher, who also disclaim any liability incurred in connection with the use of this data or specific details.

No part of this book may be reproduced without expressed, written permission from the publisher. For information about permission to reproduce selections from this book, write to: 729 Prospect Avenue, PO Box 1, Osceola, WI 54020-0001 USA

Unless otherwise noted, all photos used in this book have been reproduced from original prints made from negatives owned by William T. Kirkland.

Not endorsed or sponsored by NASCAR®.

We recognize that some words, model names, and designations mentioned in this book are the property of the trademark holder. We use them only for identification purposes.

MBI Publishing Company books are also available at discounts in bulk quantity for industrial or sales-promotional use. For details write to Special Sales Manager at Motorbooks International Wholesalers & Distributors, 729 Prospect Avenue, PO Box 1, Osceola, WI 54020-0001 USA

Library of Congress Cataloging-in-Publication Data
    Kirkland, Tom
        Darlington International Raceway, 1950–1967 / Tom Kirkland & David Thompson.
        p.   cm.
    Includes index.
    ISBN 0-7603-0692-3 (pbk. : alk. paper)
    1. Darlington International Raceway. I. Thompson, David. II. Title.
GV1033.5.D37K57   1999
796.72'06'875766—dc21   99-13101

On the front cover: In 1956, Chevrolet ran a 24-hour endurance test at Darlington. Smokey Yunick was the lead mechanic and six drivers were used — three for each car. Paul Goldsmith, Jim Reed, Fonty Flock, Tim Flock, Bob Welborn, and Betty Skelton were the drivers.

On the frontispiece: Buck Baker was one of the drivers who knew how to tame the Lady in Black, winning the Southern 500 three times— in 1953, 1960, and 1964—and finishing in the top five in 1957, 1958, and 1965.

On the title page: Joe Weatherly (12), Eddie Pagan (45), Fireball Roberts (22), and Joe Eubanks (6) run three-wide through the turn at the 1958 Southern 500.

On the back cover: Top: H.G. Rosier (5) spins out just in front of Cale Yarborough (92) during the 1962 Southern 500. Bottom: Junior Johnson and Fred Lorenzen at the 1963 Southern 500.

Edited by Lee Klancher
Designed by Rebecca Allen

Printed in Hong Kong

Contents

Dedication and Acknowledgments 7
Preface 8
Introduction 10
Chapter 1 **Darlington Raceway: A Brief History** 17
Chapter 2 **Construction** 21
Chapter 3 **1950: The Legacy Begins** 25
Chapter 4 **1951: The Hero Factor** 31
Chapter 5 **1952: Fonty's Firesuit** 37
Chapter 6 **1953: Roll Bars and the Beauty Pageant** 41
Chapter 7 **1954: Thomas Doubles Up** 47
Chapter 8 **1955: Mr. Darlington** 51
Chapter 9 **1956: Tunneling In** 57
Chapter 10 **1957: A Tragedy** 63
Chapter 11 **1958: Into the Limelight** 71
Chapter 12 **1959: Hard Drivin'** 87
Chapter 13 **1960: The Lady in Black Strikes** 95
Chapter 14 **1961: Pomp and Circumstance** 103
Chapter 15 **1962: Johnson . . . er, Frank** 111
Chapter 16 **1963: "Little Rebs" and Big "Tiny"** 119
Chapter 17 **1964: No More Monza** 125
Chapter 18 **1965: Little Joe's Legacy** 133
Chapter 19 **1966: Legends of the Lady in Black** 141
Chapter 20 **1967: The End of an Era** 145
Epilogue 150
Appendix **Race Results** 151
Index 160

Saturday morning, bright and early, loud cannons and the playing of "Dixie" will honor her. At the starting time, 38 suitors strapped in the most powerful stock cars in the world will vie for the title she offers. Only one can claim her crown....

"The Lady in Black" is many things. She is legend, she is treacherous, she is desirable, she is beautiful, and she is unpredictable.

And, too, she is the most appealing lady in the world of stock car racing.

—Benny Phillips
From the 1966 Rebel 400 Souvenir Program

Note: Because Darlington Raceway was the first superspeedway paved with black asphalt, it was called "The Lady in Black."

Dedication

*This book is dedicated
to the memory of Harold Brasington
for having had the vision to build the track
that built stock car racing.*

Acknowledgments

We acknowledge and thank the following individuals for their support of this project (listed in alphabetical order):

- Russell Branham, director of public relations, Darlington Raceway, for his cooperation and assistance in providing race results and other historical information about Darlington Raceway;
- Dr. Walter Edgar, director, Institute of Southern Studies, University of South Carolina, for inviting David Thompson (Turbo) to teach *Stock Cars and the American South*, a liberal arts course (1996) at which Tom Kirkland appeared as a guest;
- Peg Kirkland, Tom's wife;
- The late Joe Penland, a NASCAR Sportsman series champion who encouraged Turbo to research and chronicle the early days of stock car racing;
- Richard and Joan Thompson, Turbo's parents, for use of their residence in Hendersonville, North Carolina, as "headquarters" during research and writing of this book;
- Birgit Wassmuth, Ph.D., Turbo's wife, for her encouragement and support.

Opposite: Darlington Raceway, about 1963.

Preface

In April 1996, I attended a car show in Columbia, South Carolina. I was gathering material for "Stock Car Racing and the American South," a college course about the history and culture of stock car racing that I created. I thought I'd meet some race car drivers and take some pictures of a few race cars. I did that.

But, I also found a couple of folding tables on which about eight panels of peg board displayed photographs of stock car races, drivers, and crashes. Old races! Famous drivers! Spectacular crashes!

A sheet of notebook paper was stuck with masking tape to the edge of one of the tables. It said, in handmade letters, "Photos are for sale."

A quiet little man with an aging face stood off to the side. Quiet; arms crossed; patient.

"Are these your photos?"

"Yes, they are," he said.

"This is an amazing collection."

"Thank you," he said, uncrossing his arms.

"You have pictures of all the famous old drivers."

"Uh-huh," he said.

"It looks like most of these photos were taken at Darlington."

"They were," he said.

"This is great! How did you get this collection?"

"They're mine," he said.

"Okay. But how did you find all these incredible photos?"

"I didn't find them," he said. "They're mine. I took them."

"Oh my gosh, who are you?"

"Tom Kirkland," he said with a sparkle in his eye. "I was the track photographer at Darlington for quite a number of years."

Programs from the Southern 500 and Rebel 300 and Rebel 400 races from 1950 to 1967 credit his pictures with: "Tom Kirkland, Official Photographer," "Tom Kirkland, Speedway Official Photographer," or simply "Photos by Tom Kirkland."

Tom visited my stock car racing class as a guest lecturer. He brought even more pictures!

Tom seemed impressed by my analyses of his photos. And he seemed to appreciate my observations about "the early days" of organized stock car racing on asphalt.

We sensed a collaboration, and the idea for this book was formed.

Authors David Thompson and Tom Kirkland poring over photos. Unlike other track photographers, Kirkland retained ownership of his negatives. For this book, the authors selected from several hundred of Kirkland's favorites. *Birgit Wassmuth*

Tom Kirkland and his photos are the primary sources for this book. This is not a comprehensive history of stock car racing at Darlington International Raceway, now known as Darlington Raceway.

Intended to present a visual overview of stock car racing and the rituals that surround it in Darlington, South Carolina, from 1950 to 1967, this book features Tom Kirkland's black and white photographs, including several dramatic crash sequences.

To document the "photographer's eye" of Tom Kirkland, to see what he saw, and to get a feel for his sense of "capturing the moment," images of the Darlington Raceway taken by other photographers are not included in this book. The images reproduced in this book (except where indicated) are original prints made from Tom Kirkland's negatives and processed by Tom.

In the 1950s, Tom Kirkland was an innovator in the field of stock car racing photography. While others were able to take only a single photo of a spin or crash, Tom was the first professional photographer to shoot multiframe sequences of stock car racing. As early as 1958!

Four of Tom's photos were the first stock car racing pictures featured in *Sports Illustrated* magazine, September 15, 1958, ("Safe Drivers All," Pages 28–29).

Tom Kirkland's photos are a "Who's Who" of NASCAR's early heroes: Buck Baker and his son, Buddy; Lee Petty and his son, Richard; Johnny Mantz; Tim Flock and his brother, Fonty; Ned Jarrett; Elmo Langley; Tiny Lund; Hershell McGriff; Fireball Roberts; Louise Smith; Herb Thomas; Speedy Thompson; Curtis Turner; Joe Weatherly; Cale Yarborough; and many more.

NASCAR has grown because of the efforts and dedication of many people—Bill France Sr. whose leadership built the NASCAR organization; the drivers, car owners, crews and their sponsors; and the thousands of stock car racing fans, whose enthusiasm for this sport has grown exponentially since the first Southern 500 in September 1950. The hero of this book, however, is Harold Brasington, the man who built Darlington International Raceway. As Tom tells it: "Before Darlington there was dirt track racing. Then Harold Brasington came along and said, 'Let there be asphalt.' And there was asphalt."

Author David Thompson

Stock car racing has grown from a competition between moonshine runners on dirt tracks in the South to an entertainment marketing phenomenon hosted by speedways throughout the United States. Australia and Japan also have hosted NASCAR events.

The sport has changed with the times. But let's not forget where this superspeedway boom began—Darlington International Raceway and the 1950 Southern 500.

Tom Kirkland's photos provide a photographic record of this critical time in the development of professional stock car racing. His insights and observations help bring these photographs to life. He also describes some of the challenges he faced, as well as the stories behind the photographs.

I hope you enjoy this look into the past!

—David Thompson (Turbo)

Introduction

by Tom Kirkland

The year was 1939, on a hot summer day in June. Not enough neighborhood boys could be rounded up for baseball, so two of us drew a circle in the dirt for some marble shooting. Shooting marbles is pretty much a one-on-one sport. This was my best friend, and we were playing in his backyard.

We were just beginning when his older brother came out of the house holding a camera. It was really just an inexpensive Kodak. He said he had one frame left on the roll of film and wanted to use it up so he could develop the roll. In those days, nothing was wasted.

He exposed the frame—the two of us in the shooting position—and went back into the house. Neither of us seemed able to win all the other's marbles, and the game went on for quite some time.

While we were involved in our marble game, his brother developed his film, dried it by fan, and made a contact print. Out of the house he came with the print for us to see. It was still a little wet.

That was it. I was hooked.

I knew at that moment what I had to do. But in those days, nothing came easy. Where could I learn to do this? How could I get a camera, even a Kodak? I had no money. I was the ripe old age of 10.

The thought never left me, and it was a full two years later that I heard about some men in Florence (South Carolina) talking about starting a camera club—the Florence Camera Club.

If they took me seriously or looked at me as a mascot, I will never know. All I knew was I was accepted—a charter member.

At this time, I was 12 and delivering newspapers to make some money. I learned that one of my customers was also a member of the camera club. He had a darkroom in his home.

Nothing could be finer. We became big buddies, and he taught me the ins and outs of photography.

My next big thrill came when a friend asked me to go to a stock car race. I am not sure exactly where it was, but it was about 30 minutes south of Florence.

The race was run on an old horse track that was dirt and barely wide enough for two cars. They slid around the turns three abreast, and one turned over about every four laps. Once again, I was hooked.

We went to every track we could find: Columbia, Summerville, Augusta, Charlotte, High Point, Hickory, and many others. There were so many of these "bull rings," it's hard to remember all of them.

I do not know why, but I never put my two loves—photography and stock car racing—together. That is, until Harold Brasington built Darlington Raceway right in my backyard—about seven minutes from home by the back roads.

Working for the *Florence Morning News* put me at the Darlington track. Russ Catlin, who was brought in after the 1953 Southern 500 to be public relations director, needed photographs, so he and I struck a deal: I had free run of the place; I could go anywhere I wanted—with no pay—and I would furnish the track with any prints they wanted for only $1.00 per reprint. These prints were to be used to promote Darlington Raceway only, including use in the next year's souvenir program.

Then I was afforded the opportunity of marketing prints with any of the sponsor's companies. In those days, it was all companies that dealt in racing like Pure Oil Company, Firestone Tire & Rubber Company, Gabriel Shock Absorbers, Grey Rock Linings, and Falstaff Brewing Company.

The smartest thing I ever did was to demand ownership of the pictures and ownership of the negatives.

I didn't really deal much with the owners of the track. My dealings were with Russ Catlin, the public relations director. Russ was a prince of a guy, the nicest anyone could work with.

He had previously been racing editor with *Speed Age* magazine, which had been defunct for years. And he was also involved with Indianapolis. I guess it was in connection with *Speed Age* that he was involved with Indianapolis. He was involved well enough that a phone call got me two comp tickets to the 1965 Indy 500.

In the 1958 race at Darlington, that's how I got the six-picture sequence of Jack Smith jumping the rail. And that's the same camera I used to shoot the sequence of the Petty-Beauchamp finish at Daytona in 1959. I was the only one at the race that had one of these cameras.

It was a German-made camera found in the Russian occupation zone after World War II, a Praktina FX.

It had an attachment that had a spring-wound device that would advance the film.

I bought the sequence camera, the film-advance attachment, and a 135-millimeter telephoto lens by mail order. The whole thing cost $660. And I paid for it that one day at Darlington in 1958.

Magazines didn't run a lot of photos back then. *Motor Life* and *Speed Age* did run some. But *Sports Illustrated* ran four of my pictures on a double page in September 1958. That was the first time that stock car racing was featured in *Sports Illustrated*.

A writer with *Sports Illustrated*, Kenneth Rudeen, came to Darlington and told Russ Catlin that he wanted to write a story about the race, and he'd like to pick up a picture to illustrate his story. So Russ put him in touch with me. He asked how soon after the race he could get a picture. I told him that my dark room was right there. I would process film right after the race, and I could make him a quick print.

The souvenir program for the 1966 Southern 500 offers a look at photographer Tom Kirkland (left) at work. The other photographers shown are Taylor Warren (center) and Ray Mann (right).

After the race I processed the film and while the film was still in the wash, he came by, and I took it out and just strung out the 35-millimeter film. I said, "Well do you see anything you like?" He said, "My God! I want this, and this, and this, and this, and this, and this, and this." And he ended up buying 40 prints to take back to New York. And from the 40, they used four.

One of them was the picture of Eddie Pagan hitting the wall in 1958. There was no time for a second picture. The car hit the rail—Bam!—and was gone out of the track. In fact, I didn't even see the car. I never saw the wreck. I shot the picture by impulse. I heard the car, threw the camera up to the sound and clicked. And that picture has probably been published in 500 different places.

So that was the first time pictures of stock car racing were featured in *Sports Illustrated*. As a result of that, I was sent to Daytona on assignment from *Sports Illustrated* for the inaugural 1959 race in Daytona.

In that first race at Daytona, in 1959, they gave the race to the wrong man. They announced that Johnny Beauchamp had won the race. And when the race was over I went into the PR director's office at Daytona and said, "You gave the race to the wrong man." See, I had made a sequence of pictures of the finish.

He said, "No, no. No, they got it right."

I said, "Well I got pictures that'll show differently."

He said, "Well if you do, I want to see them."

So I drove home from Daytona that night. Processed the film. Didn't even look at it. Hung it up to dry. And got a couple of hours of sleep. Got up; looked at the film. Sure enough, there it was. Lee Petty was leading before the finish line, right at the finish line and past the finish line. So if he was leading in those three places, he was leading right on the finish line.

I called Daytona and told the PR director what I had.

He said, "Fine. I'd like to get them."

And he instructed me to make prints and take them out to the airport. At that time Eastern Airlines was flying Martin 404s from somewhere up the road to Miami. They made stops in Florence, Charleston, Jacksonville, and then Daytona.

I was instructed to put the pictures in an envelope and carry them on board. I was to give them to the pilot with a $20 bill and tell him . . .

I said, "Twenty dollars!"

Twenty dollars was a lot of money back then.

He said, "Yep. Give him a $20 bill."

Well, I gave the pilot a $20 bill and told him that someone would come on the plane in Daytona and pick up the envelope and give him another $20 bill.

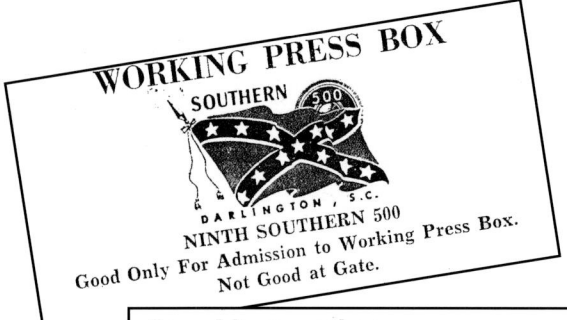

The back of a Working Press Box ticket issued to Tom Kirkland. Russ Catlin, Darlington International Raceway's director of public relations, signed it. This gave Kirkland unrestricted access to any area of the track—infield, pits, trackside, press box, scorers' stand, victory lane, or anywhere else. Most other photographers had limited access.

His eyes went wide, and he took the envelope and delivered it.

This was Monday afternoon. They judged the race and announced, on Tuesday, that the true winner was Lee Petty. They sent me a letter thanking me for the use of the pictures. That letter also said that if there were any charges I should bill Daytona.

You know what? They never paid that bill.

Actually, Daytona asked several photographers for their pictures of the finish in 1959. But to my knowledge, I was the only one who had a sequence of pictures.

You see, in the beginning, the 4x5 Speed Graphic was the standard camera. I don't know of anyone who used anything other than that in the beginning.

The 4x5 Speed Graphic was the standard camera in those days. It would make a single picture. Then you'd have to put the dark slide in. Pull the film holder out. Turn it over. Put it back into the camera. And pull the dark slide out to make another picture.

That took some time. So one picture of a wreck was all you were going to get.

Then, the 2 1/4x2 1/4 Rolleiflex came around in the early 1950s. But 35-millimeter cameras were used only for transparencies—slides—in those days.

Films available at that time were not of the quality that they were later. And making anything bigger than about a 5x7-inch print from a 35-millimeter negative was unheard of. The grain was so bad. So we went with the larger cameras to get larger negatives. From the large negatives we could make prints that were of a size and quality to really show some detail.

Then the films got better. And in 1958, I used that spring-advanced 35-millimeter camera with Plus-X film. At that time, Plus-X was a 100-speed film. It was slower than the 4x5 Tri-X, which was the 400-speed film. But, by then the lenses were better and, hence, made a better print.

So the 35-millimeter really became the standard probably in the 1960s. But there were still some photographers using the 4x5 Speed Graphics even then.

Now, today, it's common for a photographer to snap 8 or 10 frames on one situation. Back then, you snapped one shot. You made each one count. There wasn't the money back then to buy a lot of film. Not only that, but carrying enough film in the holders and carrying enough holders—I remember carrying as many as 36 holders—that weighed four times as much as the camera! You were burdened by the bulk.

We didn't use tripods back then. A tripod really wouldn't have been any good in racing. You'd have a camera on a tripod and the action would happen somewhere other than where you had the camera. You just hoped that if there was action you were in the right place to get it on film.

In the old days, I remember some photographers, including me, would shoot the beginning of the race in the Number One Turn from the outside of the track. And then, when all the cars went by, we'd run across the track to the inside. Right across the track. While they were racing!

After that first shot, I positioned myself between Turns One and Two, standing right on the edge of the track. I'd be on the grass, or the dirt, halfway between the inside guardrail and the outside guard rail. When all the cars would come by, the other photographers and I would shoot our pictures. Then we would leisurely walk back and cross over the inside guard rail.

Things were quite different in those days. Take yellow flags. Caution flags. These days they throw a caution for any little thing.

On many occasions I remember debris on the track. In those days, debris on the track had to really be debris on the track! They didn't even slow down for small pieces. And I have seen track workers look to see if the car is well away, and run out to get a piece of debris and run back with it.

They didn't get a caution flag for every little incident back then. In fact, it was hard to get a caution flag in those days. There were some teams that had a contract with one of the lesser drivers, who would wreck his car on cue, just to draw a caution so that the other team could make a pit stop.

Oh listen, this was normal back then! If they needed a caution, they'd get him to wreck his car so there would be a caution.

How did they tell him? They'd write "Now" on a pit board, a little chalk board, and hold it up to show the driver.

There was one race driver who was famous for being able to wreck a car. In 1959, they made a movie at Darlington called

Thunder in Carolina [later renamed *Hard Drivin'*]. They filmed some before the race. They did some filming during the race. And they did quite a bit of filming after the race.

One of the setup shots they were doing was where two cars would go into the Number One Turn and wreck, and one would turn over.

They had a high-priced stuntman from California, who was there doing the driving. They made five or six takes, and he wasn't able to turn the car over. The director was becoming furious.

One of the regular drivers, Neil Castles (Soapy) said, "The boy can't turn the car over. Give me a $150, and I'll turn the son-of-a-gun over."

And the director said, "You got the job."

On the first try, Soapy turned that car over and rolled it down the bank.

This guy could turn a car over in a heartbeat. He knew exactly how to do it. And he did it without endangering the driver in the other car.

Not to say that he was the one who would cause the cautions during the races.

They ran two races at Darlington almost every year. You know the early years are a little hazy on what year what happened. But the Southern 500 was run every Labor Day, beginning in 1950. And it was run on Monday.

One year, the second race was an Indianapolis-type car race. They called those "Big Cars."

And one year they had motorcycles, which was a disaster. The American Motorcycle Association sanctioned the race. They had a race scheduled at Darlington in 1951, I believe.

The AMA has racers in three categories: Novice, Amateur, and Expert. Three separate races, one for each category, would make up an event.

During that first motorcycle race at Darlington, several riders were injured, and, as I remember it, two were killed.

The track was not made for motorcycle racing. So, the American Motorcycle Association just canceled the race. The Amateurs and Experts never ran.

In 1955, they ran a Modified race.

And in 1956, they ran another Indianapolis-type car race.

In 1957 was the inaugural convertible race. This was nothing more than a Grand National car with the top cut off and a roll bar in it. The Grand National division is known now as the Winston Cup Series.

NASCAR ran the convertible division for a few years. But Darlington kept the convertible race even longer than NASCAR had its convertible division.

In those days, racing teams didn't have a stable of 8, 10, or 12 race cars. They had one race car. So when they'd come to Darlington for the Rebel 300, they'd cut the top off their Grand National cars. And when they went to the next race, they'd weld the tops back on.

So, Darlington started the convertible race in 1957, and it was known as the Rebel 300. The spring race was the Rebel race, held on Confederate Memorial Day, the Saturday nearest May 10.

I think by mutual agreement between Darlington, Daytona and NASCAR, they did away with the convertible division entirely. The Rebel race went back to hard tops in 1963. They didn't run convertibles any more. In 1966, the Rebel race became a 400-mile race.

At the time they were running convertibles, Daytona would have one 125-mile qualifying race for hard tops and another for convertibles. The top 20 cars in each division would race on Sunday. So you would see convertibles racing against hard tops.

There wasn't really any difference in the speed of the convertibles and hard tops. Back then, aerodynamics didn't play a big part in racing. It was just pure, brute horsepower. They were running 413-cubic-inch engines. Ford had a 426. Chrysler had a 413. Then Chrysler came out with a 440, the Magnum.

Unite a love of photography with a love of racing, and wonderful things may happen. I love photography and I love racing. And wonderful things did happen.

—Tom Kirkland

In the beginning, the stock car was the Modified. There was no "stock" car. They were all *modified*. They took old jalopies and put flathead motors in them. They'd put two or three or four carburetors on those engines. And they burned methyl alcohol for fuel. That's what was run on short tracks, before Darlington was built.

At Darlington, the "stock" car was born. The Southern 500 was open to the 75 fastest "strictly stock" cars. And they were inspected to be strictly stock, meaning exactly like the cars anyone could buy in a car dealer's showroom.

As I remember it, they did the inspections before the race. In the old days, the NASCAR inspectors pulled the heads of every car that entered the race to determine displacement. Before long, they figured out that checking every car took too much time. So NASCAR said, "Okay, fellas. We're going to tear down certain cars. So you better be legal. Everybody better be legal."

They didn't require much in the way of safety equipment back then. In that first race, I do not recall a car with a roll bar. I know for a fact the winner, Johnny Mantz, did not have a roll bar. He wrecked his car in practice, after qualifying for the 1950 Southern 500. As I remember it, he went to Red Springs, North Carolina, on Sunday—the day before the race—and bought a 1950 Plymouth that was literally in the showroom. He drove it to Darlington, painted the number on it Monday morning, and raced it. And won the race! And it definitely had no roll bar in it.

There really was nothing in the way of safety equipment then. Seatbelts weren't installed in every car like they are now.

Russ Catlin was Darlington Raceway's public relations director. Catlin and Tom Kirkland had a gentlemen's agreement, rather than a written contract, on Kirkland's role as official track photographer. Catlin's promotional skills elevated the public's awareness of stock car racing at Darlington, South Carolina.

Many of the drivers would secure themselves in various ways in the car. Some of them had airplane-type seatbelts. Some of them would take a bed sheet, roll it up, put it around the back of the seat, and tie it in front.

But the first thing a driver would do when he'd get in the car was take the belt off his pants and put it around the post of the window so the door wouldn't fly open.

These were "stock" cars. Showroom stock. Right out of the dealerships.

Some of the drivers did take the headlights and the taillights out. Others just took masking tape and taped across them so, if they did break, they wouldn't go flying over the track.

They didn't take anything out of the cars. All the window glass was still there. The windows would be rolled down while they raced.

I don't recall anyone ever listening to the radio in the car during a race. But I have seen drivers light up a cigarette and smoke it while they were racing.

I made a picture of a Hershell McGriff pit stop. There's one guy holding a large funnel and two men with five-gallon cans pouring gas into the car. That's the way they gassed the car then. Another man is changing the tire on the right front, and he has a cigarette hanging out of his mouth.

So Hershell had a full pit crew. But some of the drivers did not have full pit crews. And some of the drivers did not have a full complement of wheels for that race car.

As a rule, they did not change tires when they came in for a pit stop. They would come in only to get gas. That's the only reason they'd come in, unless they had a flat tire or a blow-out. Then they would come in and change a tire.

Today, they change all four tires, fill the tank with gas, clean the windshield and give the driver a drink in less than 20 seconds.

Back then, the only time they'd change a tire on a routine pit stop for gas would be if a tire was showing the cord. And there was no hurry. A pit stop might last three to five minutes.

As I say, not all the drivers had a full pit crew. So, quite often, you'd see a driver come in, turn the car off, get out, and he'd jack up the car and change the tire while some of his friends put gas in it.

Sometimes after a tire was changed on the car, the crew would take that old tire off the rim and put another tire on that rim with a tube in it. All the tires had tubes then. So crews without a full complement of wheels had to mount a tire in the pits whenever a rim was available.

To jack up the car, they would use shop jacks. They looked a lot like the jacks they use now. But it took 15 to 20 pumps to lift the car with those jacks. Today, the car is up on the first or second pump of the jack handle.

Back then, though, they did not have a place right in the center of the car where they could jack up the whole side of the car. They would jack up the front or the back. Or the front and then the back.

And I have seen some bumper jacks used—the old ratchet jack that hooked under the bumper.

But there was one team that devised a jack, a pneumatic jack, that was built into the car. When the car came into the pits, some kind of motor would deploy jacks near each wheel. The jacks would come down out of the car and push the car up off the pavement.

NASCAR outlawed that jack. This was back in the early 1960s. The Indy cars used that kind of jack for some time.

In the first races at Darlington, many, many tires were changed. Some drivers used truck tires on their cars. Most passenger car tires were four-ply tires and most truck tires were six-ply tires. That was the main difference. So the truck tires had a thicker and knobbier tread.

By 1957, Firestone was making a tire for racing. In 1957, Speedy Thompson won the Southern 500 in a 1957 Chevrolet, and he did it on four tires. He didn't have to change a single tire. His tires just did not wear out.

From the earliest races, the cars that were set up for the track had less tire wear than cars that missed the setup. They would adjust the camber for the left turn. I made a picture of Buck Baker with his car up on the aligner. That aligner was built right there at the track for adjusting the toe-in, caster and camber.

Many of the cars were driven to the track, even as late as 1959. Some of the cars were pulled to the track, connected to another car with a tow bar. And then some of the drivers started hauling their race cars on trailers. I can remember there was one area designated inside the track where all of the trailers were lined up, just like they line the transporters up today.

Of course there was no designation as to which one went where, as they do now. Today, there's a hierarchy of parking spots.

Times have changed.

Some of these drivers were real characters. Many of them had been racing before they came to Darlington. They were big names at dirt tracks like Columbia and Summerville, South Carolina, and High Point and Hickory, North Carolina.

There were the Flock brothers—Fonty, Tim and Bob. Buck Baker, Gober Sosebee, Jimmy Lewallen, Joe Eubanks. They had made names for themselves before Darlington. It was just known that if you went to one of these dirt tracks, these guys would be there.

Buck Baker was a city bus driver in Charlotte. Curtis Turner was a timber cruiser. He would fly his own plane over a tract of timber and calculate the board feet in that stand of timber. Racing was just a weekend thing for these guys.

I got to know some of these racers pretty well. Some of them would party all Sunday night and then race Monday.

These guys did party hardy. There's no doubt about it. But I never saw one of them drunk at the track.

At the track, the drivers were very accessible. Much more accessible than they are now. Race drivers today run from their cars to their motor homes and lock themselves in.

When I was at Darlington I posed the drivers for some of the pictures. They'd do anything you asked.

You know, the people made this an interesting job. In the racing fraternity, I met some of the finest people in the world. And some of the scum of the earth.

One tough part of the job was making pictures of the wrecks. Sometimes, a photographer was the first one to get to the car after a wreck. Some of that was not pleasant. Gory.

The photographers knew each other, but we didn't really socialize. We were all under deadline pressure.

I was a photographer for the Florence *Morning News* from 1953 until 1962. There were eight of us in the newsroom, and everybody was an editor. The editor, the associate editor, the managing editor, the city editor, the state editor, the front page editor, the sports editor and the chief photographer. I was the only photographer, but I was the "chief photographer."

I can see from my negatives that some of this film wasn't fixed too well. I tell you what, in those days, you did everything quick . . . and quicker.

I processed film at the track as soon as the race was over and I had made pictures of the winner.

In that darkroom I had over there at the track, the temperature was something else! It would get over 100 degrees in there. The dark room was an old storage shed. It was galvanized tin on the outside. It left a lot to be desired.

I had to carry developer and short stop. There was water in there. Running water was the only "luxury" that was afforded.

Only three of us had access to that so-called darkroom. Associated Press, United Press International, and me. It was pretty crowded. Whoever got there first got out of there first. While one's film was washing, the next one's was being developed. And while the washed film was hanging up to dry, one was washing and one was developing.

The AP photographer was Rudy Faircloth. The UPI had several from time to time. But they were headed up by Tom Price, who was the UPI bureau chief in Columbia. He later worked with the University of South Carolina as their information director.

We always got along with one another. Working in close quarters like that, you had to get along.

But that heat! It changes the chemicals to the point that we'd have to adjust the processing of any film that develops on a time and temperature basis. If a film had a normal development time of 10 minutes, that was cut down to about 2 1/2 minutes at 100 degrees.

Speaking of heat, these race cars ran some "hot" gas. The Pure Oil Company was a major sponsor of the races. Pure provided the fuel.

I remember a fellow named George Brain. He was the head man for Pure Oil at the race track. At every race he'd come to me and say, "Now when you get a chance, bring your car on over and let us fill it up for you."

That was some good gas! It was high-octane gas. It was probably 105 or 110 octane. That's even higher than airplane gas in World War II. It was only 100 octane.

By 1967, the raceway was trying to get rid of Russ Catlin. For no good reason, as far as I knew.

There were some on the Board of Directors who just didn't like him. They didn't like the idea that he was able to come in and work the race until he got everything cleaned up at the end of September, and then he was off until the spring race. He'd go down to Florida. He had a home down there. Anyway, they didn't like it that he was getting paid a year's salary and was off so much. There was a lot of jealousy.

So, they devised a plan to get rid of him. The Board of Directors would elevate him to president of the raceway and then bring in a replacement for PR director. And they had a new election and elected another president, which put Russ out.

All of a sudden, the new public relations director was giving away all of the pictures I had made for them at a nominal fee to the sponsors' companies . . . for free! That knocked me out of selling the pictures. So when Russ left, I left. And that's it. That's the story.

Pit boards and hand signals were the only form of communication between the driver and his crew chief before the advent of radios. If someone in the pits wanted to tell the driver to wreck the car and cause a caution, the traditional signal was "NOW!"

Chapter 1
Darlington Raceway: A Brief History

Before Harold Brasington built the egg-shaped Darlington Raceway, stock cars competed on dirt tracks, fairground circuits used primarily for horse racing, running tracks that circled football fields, and even baseball fields.

High-banked ovals "paved" with wooden planks were usually reserved for Indianapolis-type "Speedway" cars, otherwise known as "Big Cars."

Darlington Raceway made stock car racing history by becoming the first paved superspeedway, a track more than one mile in circumference.

As a young man, Harold Brasington, a native of Darlington, South Carolina, had loved racing. He drove to a fourth-place finish in the 1938 Daytona Beach race. But the dream to build a large, paved race course for stock cars was inspired by a trip to Indianapolis.

By then, Brasington owned a heavy equipment company in Darlington, a farming community located 10 miles west of Florence, 75 miles northeast of Columbia and 96 miles southwest of Charlotte, North Carolina.

Brasington persuaded Sherman Ramsey, another local businessman, to trade 70 acres of farmland for stock. Brasington was selling shares to raise the $50,000 needed for construction of the track.

He broke ground on December 13, 1949, at the site, one mile west of downtown Darlington on Highway 34.

According to Godwin Kelly (*Darlington: The First Superspeedway*, American Racing Classics, January 1992), Brasington "almost single-handedly carved the 1.25-mile course from Ramsey's nondescript plot, working without a master blueprint. This seat-of-the-pants engineering and Ramsey's fish pond contributed to Darlington Raceway's unique ovoid layout . . . .

"Unlike most of today's superspeedways with symmetrical dimensions, Brasington's was a bit out of balance," Kelly wrote. "The radius and banking of Turns One and Two was—and still is—completely different from Turns Three and Four. The reason was Ramsey's pond, which he wanted preserved to raise bait minnows for his frequent fishing trips."

Brasington said, "The man had a fish pond. He said, 'You miss this, and you can go to work.' We just shook hands on it. He went fishing and I went to work."

The Central States Racing Association (CSRA) had provided no more than five pre-entries for first Southern 500. So, Bill France, Sr., NASCAR's president, was asked to help. France agreed that NASCAR would cosanction the first Southern 500.

The first Southern 500 was held on Labor Day, September 4, 1950. No one was prepared for the response from racing fans. According to Harold Brasington, some fences were torn down just to allow people to get into the track more quickly.

According to Randy Riggs, author of *Flat-Out Racing: An Insider's Look at the World of Stock Car Racing*, Darlington Raceway was "smack-dab in the middle of some cotton and tobacco fields, and not the least bit convenient to motels, gas stations, major highways, or any support activity whatsoever. . . . Thirty thousand hungry-for-action racing fans endured miles of traffic and all sorts of hardships to watch the first-ever 500-mile stock car race held on a paved oval."

The first Southern 500 lasted more than five hours. Johnny Mantz won the race in a lightweight Plymouth that was easy on tire wear. His average speed was 75.250 miles per hour.

However, Al Pearce (in *The Illustrated History of Stock Car Racing: From the Sands of Daytona to Madison Avenue* by Don Hunter and Al Pearce, pages 37–38) reports controversy about the legality of the winning car. After being asked to listen to the motor of the Mantz car, NASCAR technical inspector Henry Underhill suspected an illegal cam had been used in the car.

After the race, the top five finishers were to be "torn down" for technical inspection. But Bill France, NASCAR's president and co-owner of the winning car, refused to allow the postrace evaluation. Despite the fact that illegal shocks and springs could be seen clearly, the car was not disqualified.

The protests of Underhill and "losing" drivers fell on deaf ears. Underhill resigned from NASCAR because of this apparent relaxation of the rules.

Some fans watched this race from concrete grandstands designed to hold 9,000 spectators. According to track records,

> "There is no other track on the NASCAR Grand National circuit that asks as much of a driver, mechanic and machine. An error, just one, can put a driver and race car out of the running faster than a scorer can make his mark....
>
> "There's something about the race track here. Something that drains a driver, mechanic and machine of their competitive juices. But ask Joe Weatherly and Bud Moore [winner and car owner of the seventh Rebel 400, 1963] — it gives them back when you win."
>
> By Jim Hunter,
> 1963 Southern 500 souvenir program

another 21,000 were scattered about next to the track in the turns, on the dirt embankment near the concrete grandstands, and in the infield.

By 1954, the grandstands were enlarged to seat 16,000. Attendance at the 1954 Southern 500 exceeded 40,000.

In 1955, an estimated 50,000 spectators packed themselves into the raceway.

After the 1955 race, the raceway was refenced, and another 16,000 seats were added. All 32,000 seats were sold out before the 1956 event, and 60,000 watched the race.

An archway allowed pedestrians to cross the track during the race. Some fans stood on the walkway to watch the race.

After the 1955 event, the archway was taken down, and raceway officials authorized construction of two tunnels. The tunnels allowed vehicles and pedestrians to move safely between the infield and the outside of the track. The first tunnel was built in 1956.

Also in 1956, the infield was opened on Sunday to help relieve race-day traffic jams. Spectators were allowed to camp on raceway property. Darlington Raceway promptly became known for hosting the world's largest cook-out.

In 1951, Turn One was resurfaced. In 1953, the track was expanded from 1.24 miles to 1.375 miles by rebuilding Turns One and Two. At this time, a 25-degree banking was added to these turns.

The current 1.366-mile configuration was created in 1970, when concrete retaining walls were erected around the entire track and Turns Three and Four were banked to 23 degrees.

Pre-race activities extended beyond the raceway. Darlington's police department sponsored the first Miss Southern 500 Beauty Pageant in 1953. Proceeds from the pageant were used to support the department's youth program.

Held Saturday night prior to Labor Day, the Miss Southern 500 pageant was said to have become the second largest beauty pageant in the United States.

The Southern 500 Festival was established by the Darlington Chamber of Commerce in 1957. A parade through downtown Darlington was the highlight of the festival. The parade was held Saturday prior to Labor Day.

The Southern 500 Festival started on Thursday, 12 days before Labor Day. Festival activities included parties, dances and cook outs.

In 1966, an amateur golf tournament was established. "The Southern 500 Invitational" was played at the Darlington Country Club.

The famous "Darlington Stripe" was earned, particularly in the 1950s and 1960s, by drivers scraping the guardrail in Turns Three and Four. Paint from the cars was left on the guardrail, leaving the barrier with what motorsports journalists have called the "rainbow of courage." Race cars went so fast down the back straightaway that the tail end of the car slid out and scraped the guardrail after entering Turn Three.

According to Jim Hunter's *A History of the Darlington Raceway* (1967): "The car bounces off the rail and the driver eases back on the throttle. Before he comes off Turn Four and down the main straightaway, he might have touched the guardrail two, three, maybe four times, or more."

Convertibles raced for the first time in 1957, in the inaugural Rebel 300, a race specifically for convertibles, held on Confederate Memorial Day—the Saturday nearest May 10.

NASCAR had discontinued the convertible division in 1959. But at Darlington, the Rebel race remained a "ragtop" race until

1963. The Rebel race changed format again in 1966, when it became a 400-mile race.

Hollywood came to South Carolina in 1959. *Thunder in Carolina*, the first movie with a stock car racing theme was filmed at Darlington Raceway. A camera car was entered in the race. So some filming was done during the 1959 Southern 500. Later renamed *Hard Drivin'*, the film stars Rory Calhoun and Alan Hale Jr.

Prize money for the Southern 500 increased greatly over the years. The total purse in 1950 was $25,000. By 1960, it was $90,000.

Darlington's Pure Record Club was established in 1960. Inducted into the club was the fastest qualifier for each make of car entered in the Southern 500.

Charter members were the top qualifiers from 1959's Southern 500:

Speedy Thompson, Chevrolet • Elmo Langley, Buick
Dick Joslyn, Dodge • Marvin Panch, Ford
Richard Petty, Plymouth • Fireball Roberts, Pontiac
Bob Burdick, Thunderbird • Joe Caspolich, Oldsmobile

Members of the club were to form a committee "to instruct and approve rookie drivers for the Southern 500."

Members served as official spokesmen at all events related to the Southern 500. A ring, an emblemed dinner jacket, stationery, and driving suits were awarded to new members. The induction ceremony was held during an annual banquet at the VFW Club in Florence.

Radio coverage of stock car racing from Darlington began in 1952 and was broadcast worldwide by 1962. WJMX in Florence was the Darlington Raceway Network's originating station. Paul Benson, Jr., manager and co-owner of WJMX, is credited with establishing a network of almost 300 stations, including the Armed Services Network.

The Darlington Raceway Network eventually would be sold to a NASCAR-owned enterprise known as the Motor Racing Network (MRN).

An article titled "Paul Benson: Dean of Stock Car Radio Networks" by Sadie B. Wantin in the 1962 Southern 500 souvenir program describes the network's audience:

"The fans listen for the race itself, not for accidents, [according to Benson]. He adds that among the most rabid of the fans are women—old women, young women, shut-ins—all kinds," Wantin states.

Benson, who coordinated the show, had cataracts, so he never actually saw a race.

Wantin describes, in detail, the logistics of broadcasting from Darlington Raceway:

> The first broadcast [in 1952] was from the old open pagoda (not unlike a beaten-up attic) that was so noisy that static sometimes would have seemed a welcome relief.

> Now [in 1962] 30 radio men and women are on the job—veterans in Southern 500 broadcasting and important factors in its development as an international sports phenomenon.

> The U.S. Weather Bureau has a representative on hand to talk about the weather.

> Today's air-conditioned, soundproof "eye in the sky" control center atop Grandstand A boasts the most modern facilities available. They include a teletypewriter relaying information from the press office, three telephones—one to the track system and two to the outside—and a two-channel console (control board) to put on the air reporters located at strategic points. Runners are used to relay information from various points.

> Announcers, some with walkie-talkies and some with more complex electronic equipment, are stationed at what are referred to as remote points. One remote point (any station outside of the control center is termed remote in radio jargon) is atop Grandstand B. Another is in the new pagoda in the pit area across from the "eye in the sky." Radio-equipped cars are stationed just off the track between Turns One and Two, between Turns Three and Four, and in the far pit area. An announcer in the track safety car uses a walkie-talkie.

> By coordination of all these facilities, radio listeners—around the country and even to Africa and the South Pole—are able to participate in the colorful event.

The Joe Weatherly Stock Car Museum opened at Darlington Raceway in 1965. Within six months of opening, the museum had more than 100,000 visitors.

Original exhibits included restored, actual or replica race cars, such as the 1950 Plymouth of Johnny Mantz, Buck Baker's 1950 Oldsmobile, and Jim Reed's 1959 Chevrolet.

The museum also houses the Southern Motorsports Press Association's Hall of Fame.

Blue laws that prohibited events such as stock car racing on Sunday were relaxed in 1984, according to one source, and the Southern 500 was moved from Labor Day to the preceding Sunday.

Darlington Raceway was purchased by International Speedway Corporation in 1982. Improvements continue to be made at the track.

New grandstands were added in 1997. Because the original grandstands were built close to Highway 34, the new grandstands were built on the back stretch. That meant most race fans would not be able to see the start-finish line. So, the start-finish line was moved across the track. Turn One became Turn Three and Turn Two became Turn Four.

The first race run with the start-finish line on the "wrong" side of the track was the 1997 Southern 500.

"*I grew up thinking the Southern 500 was about as important as the World Series, the Kentucky Derby, and the Indianapolis 500, all wrapped up into one.*"

—Richard Petty, *The Book of Stock Car Wisdom*

This aerial view shows how NASCAR's first superspeedway, Darlington International Raceway, was carved out of farmland

Chapter 2
Construction
by Tom Kirkland

I often wonder where NASCAR would be if Harold Brasington had not built the first superspeedway. In 1949, Bill France was promoting races run on Daytona Beach. To my knowledge, there was no thought of a speedway. Apparently, the thought of a speedway came to Bill France after he saw the success of Darlington. Nine Southern 500s had been run at Darlington before the 1959 race at Daytona.

Daytona was the second superspeedway. Then in 1960, tracks opened in Atlanta and Charlotte. Rockingham opened in 1965.

The speedway at Indianapolis had a lot of influence on Harold Brasington. That's why he started this. He went to races in Indianapolis over some eight years or so before he began construction of Darlington International Raceway. He saw what Indianapolis was doing and said he wanted to build a race track in Darlington that would not rival Indianapolis but would be in that vein. That would bring the multitudes to Darlington for stock car races.

Everybody thought he was crazy.

Then he talked some of the people around Darlington into going with him on it. He got one man to put his farm land in for his part of the track. And Harold Brasington literally built the track. I don't mean he was the head of it. I mean he got on the motor grader and moved the dirt.

There have been all kinds of stories about what happened in 1951. Apparently, there was a power struggle. And Harold Brasington was moved out. He lost out. And his baby was taken away from him.

Of course the track as you see it today is not the track that was originally built. The original track was only a mile and a quarter. There was some kind of defect with the way they built Turns One and Two. That end of the track was torn up and rebuilt. In doing so, it made the track 1 3/8 miles. This was done after the third race, in 1952.

The main grandstand on the front stretch is exactly the same grandstand that was there all the time. That concrete is the same concrete that was poured in 1950. And it's just as hard today as it was in 1950!

Eventually, they started putting a cover over the grandstand. They did it in stages. They started down at Turn One and worked back toward Turn Four. Then they tore all the cover off. Now there's no cover on the original grandstand.

Well, it was so noisy under that metal cover. The sound would reverberate. The word says it: "Re-ver-r-r-r-r-ber-r-r-r-rate." That's exactly what would happen.

So, the track at Darlington really created stock car racing as a big-time sport.

In the beginning there was dirt. In 1950, Harold Brasington came along and said: Let there be asphalt!

And there was asphalt. And it was good.

The rest is history.

Harold Brasington, left, built the speedway at Darlington. Here, he reviews blueprints during construction of the track.

"Darlington, to me, is the greatest race track in the world. Darlington lets you know if you're a driver or not."

—Fred Lorenzen, The Book of Stock Car Wisdom

Grandstands were made by pushing dirt to create a slope, then pouring wide, deep concrete "steps," upon which fans sat.

"I'd rather run on any other track than Darlington, but I'd rather win at Darlington than any other track."

—Bobby Isaac, The Book of Stock Car Wisdom

This photo was taken from the site of the original "pagoda," a building that served as headquarters for track officials, drivers, crews and the media. It was located in the infield at the start-finish line, midway down the front straightaway. The tractor-trailer truck is pointed at Turn One. Beginning with the 1997 Mountain Dew Southern 500 (August 31), the front and back straightaways were switched and Turn One became Turn Three. The original grandstands were built too close to the highway to accommodate expansion. So, the start-finish line moved to the opposite side of the track, and new grandstands were built.

1950

Chapter 3
The Legacy Begins

The first Southern 500—the first 500-mile race and the first superspeedway race for "showroom stock" cars—was held at Darlington International Raceway on September 4, 1950. A superspeedway is a paved track at which one lap (one circuit) is more than one mile in length. The race was cosanctioned by the Central States Racing Association (CSRA) and NASCAR (National Association for Stock Car Auto Racing).

Darlington's legendary and too-often deadly raceway would become known as the Lady in Black. One-lined and difficult to pass on, the track required a mix of driving skill and sheer determination to win. She was also unforgiving to those who drove too hard and crashed.

In 1950, she would begin her legacy when Buck Baker was pronounced dead by track workers after his crash in the first Southern 500. Concerned about heat exhaustion in the 500-mile race, Baker had a gallon jug of ice-cold liquid in the car with him. He crashed, however, before he had time to heat up and drink it.

Baker said, "I was running good when I got into a terrible crash that tore the car all to hell. The first guy that got to me took one look and said, 'No need to bother with Buck . . . the poor so-and-so has his head cut off!'

"The jug had busted and the stuff splashed all over my face and head. I must have looked a mess, but actually I didn't have a scratch on me."

The jug had been filled with ice-cold tomato juice.

At the ribbon-cutting ceremony for the inaugural Southern 500 in 1950, Bill France, NASCAR's founder and president, holds the microphone. Gov. Strom Thurmond, in the suit and straw hat, stands by as Mrs. Thurmond cuts the ribbon. Harold Brasington, far right, looks on.

The pace lap of the inaugural Southern 500. The pace car was an Oldsmobile convertible. Curtis Turner is on the pole in a 1950 Oldsmobile. Next to him in the front row are Jimmy Thompson in a Lincoln (center) and Gober Sosebee (closest to the fans) in an Oldsmobile. The three-abreast line-up was "borrowed" from the Indianapolis format. Seventy-five cars started the race. The "pagoda" on the right served as a sort of headquarters for media and race officials. The small tower above the grandstands was located at the start-finish line. It housed the public address system. There was no V.I.P. seating at the time.

Louise Smith registers to drive in the first Southern 500, as Harold Brasington watches. Two women registered for this race, Miss Pat Sutton (No. 54) and Mrs. Louise Smith (No. 94). "Miss" and "Mrs." were printed on the line-up sheet. Reportedly, Louise arrived at the track late and missed her chance to qualify for the race.

Walt Crawford (64), Wally Campbell (33), Bob Smith (35), Harold Kite (21), and two other drivers race four-wide down the front stretch.

Fans in the infield erected a scaffold from which to watch the race. The higher the vantage point, the better the view.

These fans built a scaffold into their convertible. This car arrived early enough to drive across the track before the race began. The arch in the background was a pedestrian walkway that crossed the track. Before tunnels were built under the track, the archway was the only way to cross the track during the race.

Right: Before the race, a vendor sells bottles of Coca-Cola to fans, one of whom has tied a program to his head for shade. The grandstands were packed. These fans are seated on the dirt embankment—beyond the edge of the concrete grandstands near Turn Four.

Race Cars in the 1950s

Hershell McGriff's car, shown during a pit stop, is a prime example of what Bill France's "strictly stock" class was all about. McGriff drove this race car from Portland, Oregon. Notice the license plate. "City of Roses" is painted on the side of the hood. "For You a Rose in Portland Grows" and a long-stemmed rose are painted on the driver's door. Hershell's name is painted on the door, too, but it's hidden behind the rearview mirror.

The headlights are covered with masking tape—not removed, just covered with tape. All the glass is in the car: windshield (before the days of shatter-proof glass); vent window; side window; rear window. The driver's window has been rolled down. There are a few decals on the side windows, probably promoting automotive brands and products.

The hubcaps, or wheel covers, were removed, but the radio antenna and windshield wipers are still in place. McGriff's entry permit for the race is in the right corner of the windshield, just below the hand of the man who is wiping the windshield. The man is smoking a cigarette and has what looks like a race program stuffed into his back pocket.

In those days, back seat passengers—not in the race, of course—could hang on to the straps that can be seen on the door posts. Look just behind Hershell's left shoulder. That was the extent of passenger restraints at the time.

Hershell is wearing a tiny helmet. These helmets looked like something a jockey might wear. Usually, they were made of leather. There was no protection for the side of the head.

Hershell is not wearing a fireproof driving suit. It looks like he's wearing a knit shirt. The Dixie Cup company was a sponsor of the race. Hershell is taking a drink out of a Dixie Cup.

There's a big canvas strap on the hood. That was probably tied around something on the inside fender to prevent the hood from flying up and covering the windshield, in case the hood latch failed from vibration or collision.

"Number 52" is painted on the roof of the car. The number is upside down when the fans read it. But right-side up to the NASCAR scorers who are in a tower in the infield.

Three crew members are fueling the car. One holds a huge funnel, while two others hold five-gallon gas cans. (At least they aren't smoking!) The man with the funnel is wearing saddle oxfords.

Two men are changing the right front tire. One's job is to jack up the car, remove the lug nuts, remove the old tire, place the new tire, tighten the lug nuts (no air-powered wrenches, by the way), and lower the jack; the other's task is to hold the tires so they wouldn't roll onto the track.

There is no barrier between the pit area and the race track. Only a white line painted on the asphalt separates the track from pit lane.

Imagine how close the cars on the track came to the crew members who cleaned the windshield and changed tires!

The winds were calm that day in 1950. The flag on top of the announcer's stand is clinging to the flag pole, probably soggy from the humid air.

Pee Wee Martin (34) makes a pit stop as Hershell McGriff (52) races past with his arm out the window. A crew member climbs over the pit wall carrying a "four-way" lug nut wrench. Chuck Mahoney (77), Fonty Flock (47), and Bill Rexford (59) speed down the front straight.

After winning the inaugural Southern 500, Johnny Mantz goes for a kiss . . . and a cigarette—not necessarily in that order.

"They started at 11 o'clock in the morning, and the race was still running when it was almost dark. You can see in this victory shot, the sky is almost dark."
—Tom Kirkland

Race-winner Johnny Mantz hasn't changed clothes. That's what he wore to drive the race.

1951

Chapter 4
The Hero Factor

Like the CSRA before it, NASCAR has become known for well-defined rules and strict enforcement of those rules. Parity has been one of NASCAR's goals from its beginning.

This systematic implementation of regulations to ensure equal opportunity may be viewed as a manifestation of "the American way." According to NASCAR, the governing body of stock car racing, drivers and mechanics are free to compete. Yet, that competition must be fair, according to the current set of rules.

Fame, glory, and cash are awarded by the sanctioning body to winners. Those who violate the rules, the "civil rights of the track," are punished with expulsion from the track, loss of points earned in previous races, or fines.

Bill France Sr. was a driver, promoter and one of NASCAR's founders. As a driver, he knew the on-track advantages of technical innovations often developed by bootleggers. The same cars driven during the week to outrun revenue agents were raced at the track on the weekend. Often, drivers who were not outlaws did not stand a chance to win.

As a promoter, Bill France Sr. understood two things about equal opportunity: 1) Without parity, car counts dwindle. When one driver wins week after week, only one driver gets paid "top dollar" for first place. If a small group of drivers seems to win consistently, then those drivers walk away with the purse. This means other drivers simply cannot afford to keep racing.

2) Some drivers were seen as heroes. At times, these heroes were symbols of the Southern struggle for freedom against an oppressive federal government that taxed their homemade liquor. Also, hometown heroes were important to postwar America.

Bill France Sr. recognized the emotional appeal of the "hero." However, when hometown drivers cannot afford to run or consistently fail to win, the fan base fades away. Spectators stop coming to the track.

As one of NASCAR's founders, Bill France Sr. promoted "strictly stock" car racing. To be allowed on the track, the car

Frank Mundy held the pole position (front row, inside) with a qualifying speed of 84.173 miles per hour. His 1951 Studebaker lost oil pressure after only 12 laps, and he finished last, in 82nd place.

must be equipped with standard showroom features—the same car any citizen could buy.

This popularized the sport. The advantage formerly held by creative mechanics, including those who built whiskey-running cars, was declared unfair and illegal. Now, mechanical innovations were made by engineers working for automobile manufacturers in Detroit.

Men and women were inspired to register their street cars for competition.

"Strictly stock" rules also attracted fans to races. Now some of their friends were racers.

Stock car racing also had a vicarious appeal. If anyone can drive, then everyone can race.

There was financial appeal, as well. Those who felt they could win a race with their street cars took to the track hoping for "easy money," the winning purse. After all, they reasoned that racing was just driving.

The second annual Southern 500 was held in 1951. Eighty-two cars started the race. More than 6 1/2 hours later, Herb Thomas was awarded $8,800 for the win.

Marshall Teague tunes up Herb Thomas' No. 92 (1951 Hudson) in preparation for the second Southern 500 on September 3, 1951.

In 1950, 75 cars started the race—lined up three-across in 25 rows. In 1951, an exception was made to allow even more cars to race: 82 cars started the race. The starting grid filled up the front straightaway, all the way back to Turn Four. The front row included a 1951 Studebaker (right), and two 1951 Hudsons.

The crowd is on its feet in anticipation as the pace car leads the way. Drivers wave to the crowd during this warm-up lap.

Pit crews watch the leaders head through Turn One on the first lap of the race. The rest of the pack makes its way past the grandstands.

Herb Thomas in the No. 92 Hudson overtakes Shorty York's No. 90 Nash on the outside. Thomas was unstoppable that day, with the second-place finisher, Jesse James Taylor, finishing a lap back and the next driver, Buddy Shuman, 9 laps back. Shorty York finished 37 laps down, in 32nd place.

Lee Connell's Pontiac crashes after completing 58 laps. He finished 80th (of 82).

Red Byron wrecked the No. 83 Dantone Racing Stable Ford on lap 368 of the 1951 Southern 500. This photo shows the archway that allowed pedestrians to cross the track. However, many spectators would stop on the bridge to watch the race.

"There's Herb Thomas taking the checkered flag in the 1951 Southern 500. It's blurry, isn't it? Well, nobody's perfect."
—Tom Kirkland

There wasn't an official "victory lane" as there is today. The driver would just stop his car and people would crowd around. They'd open the gates after the race so fans could get down on the track. There was some picture taking. But, autographs? There wasn't much autographing until recently. I mean, who wanted somebody writing his name? That's the way people thought of it back then.

—Tom Kirkland

Herb Thomas and his *Fabulous Hudson Hornet* in victory lane. It looks as though Herb's crew may have borrowed a tire from Tommy Thompson's car, No. 40. The number is painted on the tire. Thompson finished in 70th position. He completed 148 of 400 laps before a problem with a wheel hub put him out of the race.

1952

Chapter 5
Fonty's Firesuit

"Speedway cars," with no fenders and an open "cockpit," were raced at Indianapolis. A short race had been held at Darlington Raceway with AAA speedway cars in 1951, but track records indicate only the Top 10 finishers. By 1952, NASCAR had formed its own Speedway Division.

These cars raced at Darlington for the first time on May 10, 1952. Only 22 cars entered the race, so promoters organized a Grand National Division race on the same day. Buck Baker won the Speedway race, and Dick Rathmann won the Grand National race. Rathmann won $1,000 for winning the 100-mile race.

Darlington Raceway hosted a NASCAR Modified and Sportsman race on July 4, 1952.

The Sportsman Division was a step below the Grand National Division. In today's terms, the Sportsman class was similar to Busch Grand National racing. The original Grand National class evolved into the Winston Cup Series.

Modifieds were remnants of the earliest days of stock car racing. These were "jalopies" with highly modified motors. These cars usually had two or three carburetors and ran on methyl alcohol fuel. Chassis modifications were allowed, also. For example, "shackled" leaf springs were used to restrict spring travel and improve performance through turns.

It was common in the 1950s and 1960s for two divisions, or classes, to run the same race. According to race results, the two classes were treated as equal at Darlington. There was only one winner who was not a Sportsman winner and a Modified winner.

The third Southern 500 was held on September 1, 1952. Fonty Flock won that race . . . wearing Bermuda shorts.

Fonty Flock was one of three brothers. They all raced. But Fonty was considered the most flamboyant of the three. At the track, Fonty was a character, a clown, a real attention-getter. He was also a successful driver.

Banjo Matthews (16) and Johnny Patterson (58) lead the way down the back straight toward Turn Three. Some spectators saved the price of a ticket by climbing on top of farm buildings that can be seen in the background beyond Turn Two.

This concession stand in the infield advertises "Hamburg 30¢" and "Ice Cold Mellon 20¢."

Fonty Flock may have been the first of NASCAR's stars. Not only in terms of driving proficiency, but in charisma. Fonty Flock seemed to have that "star quality" that attracted and generated publicity.

Buck Baker, Lee Petty, Frank Mundy, Red Byron and others had established themselves as top drivers. But they were drivers, not necessarily charming or endearing individuals.

Getting back to Fonty's racing suit: a short-sleeved shirt and shorts. Who could blame him? It gets hot in South Carolina.

At the time, driver safety was not a big consideration. Flame-resistant driving suits were not worn. Often, an old leather football helmet was used as a crash helmet.

Seatbelts were not five-point harnesses with two shoulder straps, two lap straps and a floor strap. Some drivers bought used airplane seatbelts, just a lap belt, from World War II surplus stores. Others were known to wrap a sheet around the seat and tie it around the waist.

Multiple "major" races per year, involvement with different classes of cars, development of publicity and creation of star drivers, and safety innovations are four keys to NASCAR's success as a for-profit enterprise and to stock car racing's success as a sport.

Heroes of the 1952 Season

Tim Flock won the 1952 NASCAR Grand National Division championship and $22,890 in winnings. He would win the championship again in 1955. Between 1949 and 1961, Tim Flock competed in 187 NASCAR events. He won 39 races.

Behind the wheel he was all business. But he was known to monkey around. Jocko Flocko was a monkey that rode with Tim Flock during races. Jocko wore a small driver's suit and goggles. Apparently, Jocko was the first monkey to die from a racing-related injury. During a race, Jocko opened the trap door that allowed drivers to examine tire wear. He was struck in the head by a stone and died several days later.

Jimmy Lewallen started the 1952 Southern 500 in 20th position. Engine trouble took him out of the race after 168 of 400 laps. His 1952 Hudson recorded a 50th place finish. Sixty-six cars had qualified for the race.

Joe Eubanks drove his 1952 Hudson to a seventh place finish in the 1952 Southern 500. He was seventh in point standings for the 1952 season.

Californian Dick Rathmann won a 100-mile Grand National Division race on May 10. Rathmann would finish the season fifth in points. With 5 wins, 14 Top 5, and 14 Top 10 finishes, Rathmann went home with $11,248 in winnings for the 1952 season. In his five-year career with NASCAR, he won 13 races in 128 starts.

Truman Fontell "Fonty" Flock (14) started first and finished first in the 1952 Southern 500. He dominated the race in his 1952 Oldsmobile, leading 321 of 400 laps. In nine years of NASCAR competition, Fonty Flock won 39 of his 187 races.

Today's victory lane celebrations are carefully staged photo opportunities. Members of the press stand in assigned places and photos are taken every time the winning driver changes hats. Each hat displays the logo of a sponsor of the race. Every product or brand name seen in victory lane has bought its way into the picture. In 1952, however, Fonty was just thirsty. Coca-Cola didn't pay to have its product photographed after the race.

1953

Chapter 6

Roll Bars and the Beauty Pageant

Driver safety became a concern in 1953. After two NASCAR drivers lost their lives within a year, new rules were mandated.

By studying the condition of wrecked race cars, particularly those in which drivers had died, officials discovered two problems. When cars roll over, their roofs tend to collapse. And in a high-impact crash, the driver's seat is likely to fold forward or to break from its mountings.

To solve the problem of roof collapse, NASCAR required a roll bar to be built into stock cars. Unlike the elaborate roll "cage" found in today's race cars, a roll bar is simply a U-shaped piece of metal tubing. The open ends of the "U" are welded to the car's frame just behind the driver's seat. The curve of the tubing extends above the driver's seat, nearly to the top of the inside of the car.

The tubing is curved, rather than bent at sharp angles, to preserve the strength of the pipe. The roll bar is welded to the car's frame rather than bolted in. Bolts may break under the severe stress of a crash.

In these "strictly stock" cars, the front seat was usually a bench seat that spanned the whole width of the interior of the car. Not a bucket seat or a specially constructed racing seat, as were used in some Modifieds. If the car was a two-door model, the seat was hinged to allow passengers access to the back seat. These seats were bolted to the floor.

The high impact of a crash often caused the seat to fold forward. Sometimes, when mounting bolts snapped, the whole seat would move. Such movement influenced the effectiveness of the seat belt. It did not hold the driver. Some drivers—even those who wore strong, tight seatbelts—were thrown from their cars upon impact.

NASCAR required securing, or "locking," the seat to prevent folding. And mechanics were told to reinforce seat mounts.

If a pre-race technical inspection revealed that a car failed to satisfy the rules, mechanics had to make modifications at the track. Conditions were primitive. The pits were open, meaning there was no covered garage area where mechanics could seek refuge from blistering South Carolina heat or afternoon rain storms.

The track itself was reconfigured to help accommodate the increasing speeds of the race cars. In 1953, the track at Darlington was expanded from 1.24 miles to 1.375 miles by rebuilding Turns One and Two. At this time, a 25-degree banking was added to these turns.

No Speedway Division race was run at Darlington in 1953. Junior Johnson won the Modified and Sportsman race in July. Buck Baker won the Southern 500 on Labor Day, driving an Oldsmobile sponsored by Griffin Motors.

Griffin Motors was a car dealership located in Florence, South Carolina, about 16 miles from the track at Darlington. The Griffin Motors entry was considered a local favorite.

In 1953, the Miss Southern 500 beauty pageant was established. The pageant was sponsored by the Darlington Police Department, and proceeds were used to support the Darlington Youth Activities fund.

Martha Dean Chestnut of Conway, South Carolina, was crowned the first Miss Southern 500. Chestnut later represented South Carolina in the Miss America pageant.

Miss Southern 500's duties included posing with the winning driver during the victory celebration. Often, the first post-race photos were taken as the driver kissed the "trophy queen."

Today, Miss Winston Cup reigns over victory lane. She is not the winner of a pageant, however. Beauty queens have been replaced by attractive, professional marketing representatives.

NASCAR still studies wrecked race cars, discovers new ways to improve driver safety, and implements rule changes to assure compliance with safety guidelines.

The pits prior to the 1953 Southern 500. Pre-race ceremonies included presentations of trophies to the pole winner and fastest qualifier. The flatbed trailer attached to the truck driving the "wrong way" on the track served as a portable stage. Between the "stage" and that truck in the background is a pickup truck pulling a sweeper. As the truck drives along, the track is brushed clean of dirt and debris.

The line-up. On the front row are Fonty Flock (14), Joe Eubanks (82), and Dick Rathmann (120). All drove Hudsons.

The Hudson Hornet was the first street car designed with aerodynamics in mind, according to John Craft, *Vintage and Historic Stock Cars*. The stock flathead, in-line six-cylinder motor was not incredibly powerful, but the body design created little aerodynamic drag, which improved speed.

Hudson created several factory stock options that were considered legal by NASCAR, including dual carburetors option and "export" axle ratios.

Hudsons recorded 73 NASCAR wins between 1951 and 1953. The 3,600-pound Hudsons had column-shifted three-speed manual transmissions. The stock motor produced 210 horsepower.

Lee Petty and his 1953 Dodge.

Lee Petty was NASCAR's first three-time Grand National champion. He earned the honor in 1954, 1958, and 1959. He won the pole 18 times and won 54 races. In a photo finish, Lee Petty edged out Johnny Beauchamp for the win at the first Daytona 500 in 1959. Petty was awarded the win three days after the race. According to Frank Moriarty, *The Encyclopedia of Stock Car Racing*, Lee Petty's career average finishing position of 7.6 is still a NASCAR record.

Called the "patriarch of the first family of stock car drivers," Lee Petty left a legacy that lives on with the driving careers of son Richard, grandson Kyle, and great-grandsons Austin and Adam.

Dick Rathmann's Hudson (120), Gober Sosebee's Oldsmobile (51), Bob Weatherly's Plymouth (50), Matt Gowen's Plymouth (99) and Fred Dove's Ford (71).

Fonty Flock was on the pole for the 1953 Southern 500, held on September 7. Fonty had dominated the 1952 Southern 500 by winning from the pole.

Known in racing circles as "Mr. Pepsodent" and the Clown Prince of NASCAR, Fonty's smile and sense of humor were a welcome presence at any track.

His first racer was a Soapbox Derby car. He won national championships in 1947 and 1949 driving Modifieds. According to Larry Fielden, in *Tim Flock: Race Driver*, Fonty became a fan favorite when he flipped his Modified at Lakewood Speedway in Atlanta. He climbed out of the car, got some help from fans to roll the car back onto its wheels, and won the race.

Hershell McGriff (5) and Fonty Flock (14) both have their rear windows down in order to tie the door to the door post. This was to prevent the driver's door from opening during the race.

Below
These trucks were filled with 105- to 110-octane racing fuel. George Brain, the "head man" at the track for Pure Oil, would tell Tom, "Now when you get a chance, bring your car on over and let us fill it up for ya."

Buck Baker (87) wins the 1953 Southern 500 as he passes (again) Buddy Shuman (89) and Gene Comstock (8). Buddy finished 14th; Gene finished 18th.

In 1953, the Miss Southern 500 Beauty Pageant was established. Sponsored by the Darlington Police Department, the pageant was held Saturday night before the race on Monday. One of Miss Southern 500's "duties" was to greet the winner in victory lane with a hug and kiss. Buck Baker is the first to take advantage of the new ritual. Miss Martha Dean Chestnut was the first Miss Southern 500. She went on to the Miss America contest as Miss South Carolina.

Buck Baker's car sits astride the Bender Magnetic Wheel Aligner. Drivers and mechanics used this device to perform front-end alignments on their race cars. A proper race setup saved tire wear and improved handling.

1954

Chapter 7
Thomas Doubles Up

The making of a legend began as Herb Thomas drove to victory in the 1954 Southern 500. Of the five Southern 500s, Thomas had won two of them.

In addition to the Southern 500, Darlington hosted an AAA Speedway Car race—which Manuel Ayulo won—and a Modified and Sportsman race, which Fireball Roberts won on July 4 with a Cadillac-powered Modified.

The car Roberts drove to victory—a lightweight Modified chassis with a Cadillac power—embodied stock car racing's outlaw origins. Moonshiners would modify their cars in order to outrun federal agents. These bootleg cars included features that were outlawed by NASCAR's "strictly stock" rules but were allowed in the Modified class (which actually preceded strictly stock), where modifications were essentially unlimited.

These features included stiff rear springs (sometimes the springs were "shackled" to lower the car's center of gravity), dual shock absorbers, oversized tires, heavy-duty wheels, and reinforced front suspension parts.

The powerplant of choice in those days was the large-displacement Cadillac engine. Bootleggers and racers would scour junk yards for Cadillac ambulances for their high-powered motors and heavy-duty suspension parts.

The Modified class racers didn't stop with stock Cadillac motors. Racing cams and multiple carburetors were used, along with race fuel—a mix of high-octane gasoline, methyl alcohol, and—occasionally—a bit of nitro methane as well. Good tuners with deep pockets made lots of horsepower, and brute horsepower won races. This kind of competition was exactly what Bill France was trying to reduce when he created the strictly stock class.

The strictly stock class drew thousands of spectators, and Darlington Raceway continued its expansion in 1954. The grandstands were enlarged to seat 16,000. The infield continued to be filled up with fans willing to brave the dust and grime, with more than 40,000 fans present to watch the fifth annual Southern 500. Herb Thomas won, with an average speed of 94.93 miles per hour. The event lasted 5 hours, 16 minutes, and 1 second.

According to Greg Fielden's *Forty Years of Stock Car Racing* series, two innovations became available to improve driver safety in 1954. A fire-resistant coverall was developed and sold to racers. This helped put an end to driving outfits like Fonty Flock's Bermuda shorts.

The other new-for-1954 feature was a helmet designed specifically for absorbing shock. This replacement for the leather hats of the day was the prototype for today's racing helmets.

Both of these innovations seem to have been adapted from military applications. Navy and Air Force pilots needed such flameproof flight suits, or coveralls. And a version of the new helmet was worn by flight crews.

In addition, the first tire developed specifically for stock car racing was introduced. According to Fielden, the Pure Oil Company introduced an all-nylon cord tire for stock cars in 1954.

A mechanic well-known for bending NASCAR rules has told the author that tires were not easy to come by in the early days of racing. As the nation continued to recover from World War II, tires were still semiprecious commodities.

Some drivers and their mechanics may admit now to their creative problem solving regarding acquisition of race rubber. As they would pass through towns on their way to a race track, they might happen to spot decent tires on a car parked on the street—and "borrow" them.

Ten crew members refuel this car during a pit stop at the Modified division race held at Darlington. To prepare these cars for racing, the gas tank was removed from under the car and mounted in the trunk. One crew member stands on top of the trunk to dump gas into the filler tube. From the shirts they wear, this could be a "pick-up" crew. This driver got help from men from Virginia and North Carolina. Notice the open hub on the wheel perched on the wall. This photograph was taken during the 1955 race.

Fireball Roberts (M-3) leads the pack into Turn One at a Modified race. Many seats were empty . . . as was the photographers' stand. Perhaps the Grand National division cars and drivers that ran the Southern 500 races had become more popular, already.

This Ford F-8 wrecker recovers the "Florida Jalousie" from the track. The driver, Ralph Moody (according to the name painted on the car), is still in the car holding the steering wheel straight for the tow back to the pits.

Modified Division Cars

Early stock cars were sometimes built by moonshiners. These entrepreneurs would "modify" their cars in order to outrun federal agents. These bootleg cars included features that were outlawed by NASCAR's "strictly stock" rules. Eventually, some of these features—designed to improve the car's handling and performance through curves at high speeds—were allowed.

These features included: stiff rear springs (sometimes the springs were "shackled" to lower the car's center of gravity), dual shock absorbers, oversized tires, heavy-duty wheels, and reinforced front suspension parts.

A class of stock cars called Modifieds had preceded the strictly stocks. Modifieds were lightweight coupes powered by flathead eight-cylinder motors.

Modifieds were "open class" cars. In other words, unlimited modifications were permitted. Racing cams were used. This engine part forces the valve lifters to open farther than a stock cam would allow, which results in a larger combustion chamber inside the cylinders. In other words, more power.

Another common feature of Modifieds is multiple carburetors. Three or four carburetors on one motor were common. Also, strictly stock cars ran on high-octane racing gasoline. Modifieds burned methyl alcohol, sometimes with a little nitro mixed in.

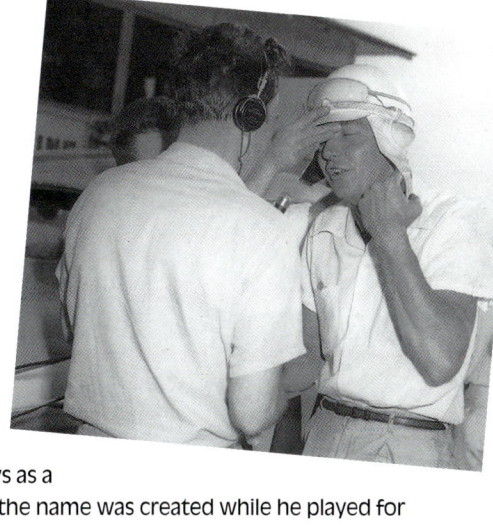

Hot, tired and happy, Fireball Roberts responds to a radio reporter's questions.

Edward Glenn Roberts Jr. was a loner. He has been described as moody and selfish. Motorsports journalists made the most of his nickname, "Fireball." But the name did not come from his speedy performance on the track. It came from his days as a fastball pitcher. Some say the name was created while he played for the Zellwood Mud Hens, an American Legion team in Florida. Others say he got the name while studying at the University of Florida.

Fireball Roberts ran only 34 Grand National events between 1950-1955. He preferred the Modified circuit, which ran races as often as six nights a week.

It is difficult to tell if the fence marks a post-race technical inspection area or an official victory lane. However, this is the first photo presented in this book that shows a physical barrier between car and driver and the crowd.

Fireball Roberts' number M-3 Modified had four carburetors on an eight-cylinder flathead Cadillac motor. He took home $1,880 for the win.

I do not know what happened to the 1954 negatives for the Southern 500. So 1954 is pretty much a wash.

—Tom Kirkland

Right
Herb Thomas celebrates his victory in the fifth Southern 500 (September 6, 1954). A winner would park the race car on the track near the start-finish line to accept the checkered flag. Fans, such as the young man in the foreground, came out of the grandstands or infield to join the victory lane festivities.

1955

Chapter 8
Mr. Darlington

The Darlington International Raceway Corporation Board of Directors had named Robert E. Colvin president of the speedway in 1952. According to Tom Kirkland, Harold Brasington had been pushed out of the position.

Bob Colvin had been "charged with the responsibility of nursing the Southern 500 into a successful maturity." He was proving himself worthy of the task. By 1955, he was known in Darlington County as "Mr. Darlington." He was a bald man whose nickname was "Curly."

Under Colvin's direction, the track's reputation for bringing class and respectability to stock car racing was continuing to grow. The Southern 500 was referred to as the Kentucky Derby of stock car racing.

His lifestyle reflected that sense of class and respectability. He had earned a master's degree in chemistry, taught at the college level, and served in the U.S. Navy during World War II.

Now, he was an active member of the community. He held leadership positions with several civic organizations, including the March of Dimes, the Elks, the Youth Movement, the Lions' Club, and more.

Colvin loved fast cars and had a passion for racing. And he saw a positive social value in racing.

"I like stock car racing and the Southern 500," Colvin said. "Out of this activity and this race come better automobiles for you and me to drive. We, Darlington, make this possible, so how can we lose?"

The Southern 500 was attracting the nation's attention. Live coverage of such an event was unheard of in the early

Here's the start. See the pace car coming off? Right dead at me! That's the way they did it. The pace car came down the front straight and off the track in Turn 1. I'm between the guard rail and the track. The pace car actually went to my right — between me and the guard rail.

—Tom Kirkland

The front-row qualifiers for the 1955 Southern 500 featured two Buicks and an Oldsmobile in a race that featured intense competition between brands. Fireball Roberts (M-1) put a Fish Carburetor Buick on the pole with Buck Baker's Buick (89) next to him on the line and Speedy Thompson's Oldsmobile (87) completing the front row in a second Buck Baker car. Of the three, only Baker would finish in the top 10. Roberts crashed out early and Thompson's suffered vapor lock about halfway through the race.

days of television. But radio coverage was enjoying a growth in syndication.

In 1952, WJMX in Florence, South Carolina, provided a network feed to three South Carolina stations. By 1955, station manager Paul Benson reported that "stations from Florida to Virginia were on the network."

A radio booth referred to as the "Eye in the Sky" had been constructed on top of the covered section of grandstand. Two vans were positioned on the apron of the track, between the racing surface and the infield guardrail. Commentators provided "eye-witness" reports from a position near an incident.

This innovative coverage helped build nationwide coverage of NASCAR events. By 1956, Benson expected to feed race coverage to an expanded network, including stations in Alabama, Louisiana, Kentucky, Ohio and Illinois.

At the 1955 the Southern 500, more than 50,000 spectators saw Herb Thomas win in a Chevrolet. This was Chevrolet's first victory in a 500-mile race.

Tim Flock stands in front of his Mercury Outboard Motor Company's Chrysler 300, owned by Carl Keikhaefer. The first multicar team owner, Keikhaefer rented an abandoned airport and used it as a testing ground for his race cars. By sponsoring race cars, Keikhaefer advertised his boat motor company. Tim Flock received his winnings and "deal" money. Tim Flock ran 187 races in his NASCAR Grand National Division career. He won 40 races and was champion in 1952 and 1955.

According to NASCAR records, Slick Smith (14) left the race after 77 laps with a blown gasket. He was paid $50 for finishing 61st (of 69).

Fonty Flock spins out of the race. Despite only completing 190 laps, he pocketed $1,040 for his efforts that day.

Fonty Flock crashed out one of the Carl Kiekhaefer Chryslers in the 1955 Southern 500. Kiekhaefer owned Mercury Outboards, a company that made boat motors. To promote his business, he sponsored—and managed—what is known as the first multicar stock car racing team. The team's cars were hauled in trucks, at a time when many race cars were driven to the track, and maintained by a crew of mechanics when a driver often doubled as chief mechanic. The Kiekhaefer trucks were known to house "full" machine shops. When others went home with broken parts after practice or qualifying, the Kiekhaefer team fabricated some replacement parts right there at the track. Kiekhaefer paid his drivers well, and he expected them to win.

There's a car spinning out, and I'm shooting a picture. And there's a photographer with his 4x5 Speed Graphic down by his side.

He was the chief photographer for the State, the newspaper in Columbia, South Carolina. He could have been making a picture, too. It's not as though he didn't see the spin. He's looking at it!

I caught me some flak for that picture. One of our compatriots chastised me for printing that picture showing another photographer in a bad light.

—Tom Kirkland

Coming off a win at Raleigh Speedway on August 20, Herb Thomas won his third Southern 500 in 1955.

Herb Thomas won the 1955 Southern 500 in a Chevrolet. Darlington Raceway always had a get-together for press, radio and so forth some time before the race — like in June, July, or August. They would invite the press, and they would usually have one of the celebrity drivers there.

In 1955, they had Herb Thomas. He stood up for all the people, and he said, "I'm going to be in Darlington for Labor Day. I'm going to win the race. And I'm going to do it in a Chevrolet."

Everybody's jaw dropped when he said that. They thought he was crazy. Driving a Chevrolet! They broke down a lot.

He did exactly what he said.

—Tom Kirkland

The Victory Dinner

The first and last victory dinner was held in 1955. Basically, the management at Darlington was trying to adopt an Indianapolis tradition. Indianapolis did not hand out awards the day of the race. They did that at a victory dinner the next day.

Herb Thomas won the sixth Southern 500 in 1955. They had him and all the other drivers stay for that dinner. The drivers were very upset at having to stay in town until the next day to get their money.

Before this, Darlington had written checks right after the race. Each driver would go into the office, sign for his check, and also sign his name on a form thanking the company that sponsored the particular laps that he led, if any.

Companies paid a cash bonus to the drivers that led the laps they sponsored.

That victory dinner really made the drivers mad.

Most of these drivers had other jobs. They missed work by staying in Darlington long enough to collect their winnings. Besides, they needed to get home and work on their cars before the next race.

Thunderbird was the official pace car of the sixth anniversary of the Southern 500. So a big photo of a Thunderbird was displayed behind the head table.

Anyway, that was the first victory dinner. And the last.

—*Tom Kirkland*

1956

Chapter 9
Tunneling In

Sixty thousand spectators watched the 1956 Southern 500. The race was sold out long before the event. An additional 16,000 seats had been added after the 1955 race. That brought the total grandstand seating capacity to 32,000. The other 28,000 fans crammed into the infield to watch, hear, smell, taste and feel the race.

Racing fans love more than fast cars. All five senses are engaged by watching stock cars. They roar past in a blur of speed, ripping through air as they go, leaving behind the smell and taste of glowing metal from the engine, clean exhaust, and hot rubber.

Stock car racing is one of the only sports that spectators truly feel. The thump of a fly ball hitting an outfielder's glove, the whoosh of a golf club swing, or the grunts of a football player just do not compare to the sensual experience of stock car racing.

When the cars fire up at the "Start your engines" command, the sound penetrates the body of each and every race fan. They can feel the sound bombard their chests. For fans, an adrenaline rush begins before the cars ever move.

Not all the fans who had watched Southern 500 races from the infield parked there. Some parked outside Darlington Raceway and used a pedestrian archway to access the infield.

The archway had allowed pedestrians to walk above the track during the race. At the time, it was the only safe way to cross the track during an event. Some fans stood on the walkway to watch the race.

However, after the 1955 Southern 500, the archway was taken down, and raceway officials authorized construction of a tunnel. The tunnel allowed vehicles and pedestrians to move safely between the infield and the outside of the track. A second tunnel was added in the 1960s.

Before the tunnels were built, the only way to get an ambulance out of the infield was to red flag the race. Races had to be stopped before emergency vehicles were allowed to cross the track.

The first tunnel was built in 1956. Construction went smoothly, although not without tragedy.

Two passenger cars attempted to jump over the gaping trench that had been dug for the tunnel and crashed. The first one made it. The second car had attempted the jump but failed. A passenger in the second car was killed. Reportedly, a third car had been present but its driver drove away without attempting the jump.

Also in 1956, the infield was opened on Sunday, the day before the Southern 500, to help relieve race-day traffic jams. Spectators were allowed to camp on raceway property. Camping at the track became a NASCAR tradition, and Darlington Raceway became known as the host of the world's largest cook-out.

Darlington's tunnels to the infield were a feature that spread to other NASCAR tracks. Testing, qualifying, and racing can proceed without interruption. This is safe, convenient, and cost effective.

A 24-hour performance test was conducted by Chevrolet at Darlington Raceway in 1956. The goal was to drive 2,400 miles in 24 hours.

A team of six drivers drove two 1956 Chevrolets 2,430 miles in 24 hours. The drivers were Jim Reed, Betty Skelton, Tim Flock, Fonty Flock, Paul Goldsmith, and Bob Welborn.

Results of this successful test were used by Chevy and its advertising agency to promote the durability and performance of the car.

Curtis Turner won the 1956 Southern 500. The victory celebration took place on the track. NASCAR officials wear striped "referee" shirts. Turner is on his car with his trophy. The beauty queen, Miss Southern 500, Robin Williamson, is standing on the hood of the race car. It was expected that the beauty queen would reward the winner with a hug and a kiss. According to the 1957 souvenir program, Miss Southern 500 must fulfill "her duty of making a lover boy out of each Darlington winner." The program also said, "Last year Miss Robin Williamson puckered for Curtis Turner in what now stands as a new record for long-distance bussing."

This Kiekhaefer Chrysler 300 crashed in a private practice session. Kiekhaefer owned Mercury Outboards, a company that made boat motors. To promote his business, he sponsored — and managed — what is known as the first multi-car stock car racing team. The team's cars were hauled in trucks at a time when many race cars were driven to the track. The Kiekhaefer cars were maintained by a crew of mechanics at a time when a driver often doubled as chief mechanic. And the Kiekhaefer trucks were known to house "full" machine shops. When others went home with broken parts after practice or qualifying, the Kiekhaefer team fabricated some replacement parts right there at the track. Kiekhaefer paid his drivers well, and he expected them to win.

Dink Widenhouse lies on the track after a multicar accident in the 1956 Southern 500. He was not seriously injured.

Dink Widenhouse (B-29), Roy Bentley (50) and Fireball Roberts (22) were involved in this accident. With the race under the yellow caution flag, two other cars drive past the wreck.

The Big Cars Come to Darlington

For 1956, the folks at Darlington looked to get back to having several races during the season. Attendance at the Modified and Sportsman races had declined, which led to that race being dropped for 1955. The following year, that race was replaced with a Speedway car race, the PeeDee 200.

The Pee Dee 200, named after South Carolina's Pee Dee region, was run on July 4, 1956, by United States Auto Club (USAC) Big Cars. Dick Rathmann, winner of the 1952 NASCAR Grand National race on May 10, finished 15th in the 1956 Pee Dee 200. It was the last time Indianapolis-type cars would run at Darlington Raceway.

On July 4, 1956, the Speedway division, also known as "Big Cars," raced at Darlington International Raceway. They had run races at Darlington in 1950, 1951 and 1954.

Johnnie Parsons won the 1950 event in the Russo-Nichels Special, averaging 104.651 miles per hour for the 200-mile race. The 1951 250-mile event was won by Walt Faulkner. The 1954 race was won by Manuel Ayulo in the Schmidt Special, averaging 123.012 miles per hour.

The Schmidt Special, from St. Louis, is pushed into place on the starting grid. The Schmidt Special had won the 1954 Speedway car race at Darlington with Manuel Ayulo at the wheel. In the 1956 race, the Schmidt Special was driven by Johnny Thompson to a 9th-place finish from a 15th-place starting position.

Pat O'Connor, winner of the Pee Dee 200 (July 4, 1956), sits on the headrest with his feet in the car to receive his trophy. A piece of sheepskin pads his shoulder harness.

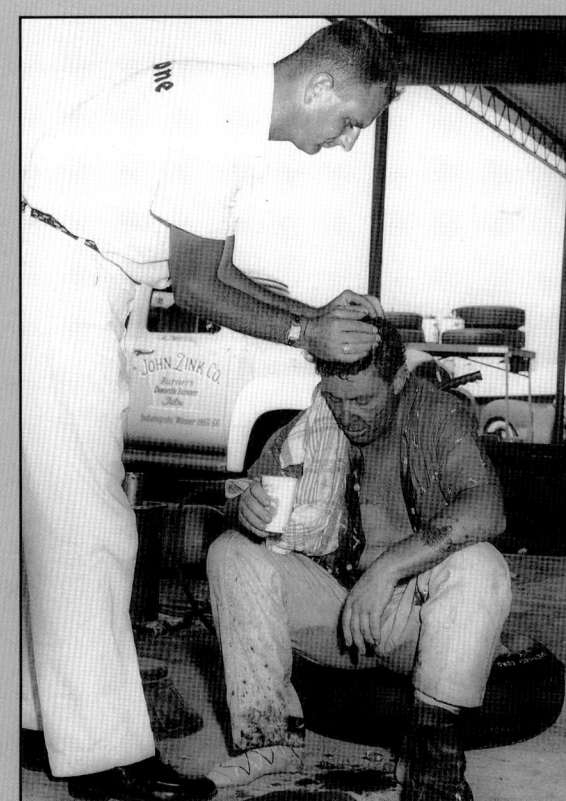

This driver is suffering more from heat exhaustion than losing the race. Ice is held on his head to cool him quickly. Notice the tire wear. He must have been fighting to steer his Big Car through the corners.

The Tunnel Tragedy

Darlington didn't always have a tunnel under the track for cars and trucks to drive through. Originally, a gate was opened before and after the race. Cars and trucks could drive across the track to the infield. But once the gate was closed, vehicles had to stay in the infield until the race was over.

There was an arched walkway so pedestrians could cross over the track during the race.

Eventually, Darlington's management decided to take down the pedestrian archway, tear up a portion of the track, and build a tunnel. Today, there are two tunnels under the track.

When they were building the first tunnel, in 1956, there was a gaping hole in the track where they had cut the trench for the tunnel.

Construction crews had poured concrete for the sides of the tunnel, but they had not built the top of the tunnel.

Three cars got onto the grounds one night. These jokers decided to jump the trench.

I got aerial pictures of it the next morning; two of the cars are still there.

This aerial photograph was taken the day after several guys tried to jump the chasm dug when the tunnel under the track was built. Note the skid marks behind the car that made the jump.

This is what is left of the car that made the jump and cleared the tunnel trench.

This is what happened to the car that didn't make it.

The track called me as soon as they found out. They didn't "find out" about it. They found it!

The young men said they were just trying to jump it. That's all. Just a lark.

One car made the jump. Another driver decided against it too late to prevent the car from flying into the pit. The third driver saw what happened to the other two and drove away.

Here's what happened. They were coming along, one behind the other. The guy driving the car that ended up at the bottom of the trench saw that the one in front of him crashed at the end of the jump. He hit his brakes and slid sideways.

Off one edge of the hole, he flew sideways right into the other side! See the round tire marks he made when he hit?

And there's one metal bar sticking straight out of the asphalt—even with the top of the tunnel and perpendicular to the pit. That's one of those metal rods they use to reinforce road surfaces. It stuck in the window and went right through the passenger's head.

'Nuf said.

—Tom Kirkland

The Endurance Test

Chevrolet held an endurance test at Darlington in 1956, planning to use two cars and drive 2,400 miles in 24 hours.

At one point, one of the cars developed some engine trouble. Smokey Yunick, who was the top mechanic at this test, diagnosed the problem just by listening to the car as it drove by on the track.

He held up a pit board to tell the driver to stay on the track and keep running.

Smokey went to a rental car that was parked on the infield and took the valves off the right side of the motor. He called the car in from the track and exchanged those valves.

That car finished the endurance run.

And they made it. Twenty-four hundred miles in 24 hours.

Six drivers were used—three for each car. Paul Goldsmith, Jim Reed, Fonty Flock, Tim Flock, Bob Welborn, and Betty Skelton were the drivers.

Both cars ran at the same time, but they started an hour apart. I shot pictures of each one as it completed the test.

—Tom Kirkland

At the end of 24 hours, the score board shows more than 2,430 miles driven. According to a story printed in the *Florence Morning News*, Bill France Sr. threw the checkered flag to signal the end of this Chevrolet endurance run.

Speedy Thompson takes the checkered flag during qualifying for the 1956 Southern 500. He put a Carl Kiekhaefer Chrysler on the outside of the front row and picked up a position to finish second. Marvin Panch qualified second and finished third.

1957

Chapter 10
A Tragedy

In 1957, convertibles raced for the first time at Darlington Raceway, in the inaugural Rebel 300. The race was held on Confederate Memorial Day—the Saturday nearest May 10.

Traditionally, stock car races featured a "flying start"—a pace lap followed by a rolling start. However, the Rebel 300 format featured a standing start. This is similar to the Indianapolis or drag racing practice of holding the cars in a starting grid until the green flag drops. Race officials thought this would be dramatic.

Another Indy idea that Darlington adopted was elevated fuel tanks, which were brought in to speed up the painfully slow process of filling the car's tank with one-, two-, or five-gallon cans and a funnel. Big steel drums, probably with a 55-gallon capacity, were placed on top of wooden frames in each driver's pit space. A hose that ran from the steel drum was inserted into the car's fuel tank, and gravity forced fuel into the race car.

This was a much faster, more efficient way to refuel during a pit stop. It was also much more dangerous.

According to Tom Kirkland, one of those fuel drums caught fire during the first Rebel 300. Before the 1957 Southern 500, NASCAR had modified its rules for refueling.

There was no mention of the Rebel 300's fuel drum fire in the 1957 Southern 500 souvenir program. But an article did describe the revised rules for refueling. No "elevated gasoline drums or refueling towers" were allowed.

No more than 30 gallons of fuel was allowed in the pit area at a time. Ten-gallon gas cans could be constructed by welding two five-gallon cans together. Approved ventilation and flexible

Joe Weatherly was a motorcycle racing champion before turning to stock cars. He won the NASCAR Grand National championship in 1962 and 1963.

A winning driver, Weatherly said, "If you want to cash in, you've got to be there when the man begins passing out the money."(from *The Book of Stock Car Wisdom*)

Traditionally, stock car drivers are superstitious. Taboos include peanut shells at the track and the color green, particularly green race cars.

Weatherly was so superstitious that he would not accept green money for winning the 1960 Rebel 300. Reportedly, he insisted on being paid the $9,250 purse in silver coins.

On May 12, 1957, the first Rebel 300 was held. This was the first convertible race at Darlington. The race began by featuring an "all star" front row of top qualifiers: Paul Goldsmith, Joe Weatherly, and Curtis Turner. A simple roll bar was welded into the convertibles. If the car turned upside down, the roll bar held the weight of the car and prevented it from crushing the driver. It looks as though Curtis Turner (No. 26) had some form of shoulder harness. It is draped over the top of the roll bar so he won't sit on it when he gets into the car.

Southern 500s were run on Labor Day. That's always a Monday. It was illegal to run a race in South Carolina on Sunday. The state's Sunday blue law would did not permit it.

But, the first Sunday race in South Carolina was the convertible race in 1957. It was scheduled for Saturday, and it was rained out.

Bob Colvin announced that it would be run the next day — Sunday.

The moment the green flag dropped and the race began, Colvin was arrested!

— Tom Kirkland

(According to the 1960 souvenir program (p. 108), Bob Colvin drove the pace car for the 1957 Rebel 300. The race began, and Colvin pulled into the pits where Sheriff Grover Bryant served him with a warrant. Reportedly, Colvin said, "Do your duty, Grover. I started the race, now you stop it!" The race went on.)

The "two-horsepower" (HP2) "Terrizasoff" (pronounced "tear his ass off") car was involved in a multicar pile-up in which the 20 car clobbered the back end of another car. The wreck blocked the front straight. The race was red-flagged. All cars stopped on the track while track crews removed crashed cars and debris from the racing surface. This was the first red-flag incident at Darlington Raceway. The race was delayed by more than an hour, according to the 1960 souvenir program.

Billy Myers (14) spins to greet Joe Weatherly (12). Weatherly ended up finishing 20th in this running of the Rebel 300.

filler tubes were required. And only one fuel can was to be used at a time. No more groups of people around the gas tank holding funnels and pouring high-octane gas.

Pre-race events became more elaborate over time. The Southern 500 Festival was established in 1957.

Organized by the Darlington Chamber of Commerce, the Southern 500 Festival started on Thursday, 12 days before Labor Day. Festival activities included parties, dances, cook-outs, and the Miss Southern 500 beauty pageant. A parade through downtown Darlington was the festival's highlight. The parade was held Saturday prior to Labor Day.

The 1957 Southern 500 souvenir program includes a list of quick facts about the history of the Southern 500, including: "Racing authorities point to Darlington Raceway to prove that the higher the banks the safer the track. Only one driver has ever been hospitalized overnight in seven runnings of the Southern 500. None fatally injured."

[Note: According to Tom Kirkland, two American Motorcycle Association racers were killed at Darlington Raceway in about 1951. But that was before the track was enlarged.]

In June 1957, the Board of Directors of the Automobile Manufacturers Association (AMA) recommended that the industry, as a whole, divorce itself from support of any kind in racing or other events that featured speed and horsepower. Spectators had been seriously injured at Martinsville, when a stock car flew over the wall and into the crowd.

Already concerned with exaggerated advertising claims about safety and speed, and fearing negative public reaction to the Martinsville incident, auto manufacturing executives decided to pull out.

Bill France took countermeasures, and races were held without interruption.

However, Darlington Raceway would record its first NASCAR fatality during the 1957 Southern 500, when 33-year-old Bobby Myers was killed when he crashed into Fonty Flock's car. No doubt about it. Driving fast is dangerous, even in the controlled conditions of a race track.

Advertising agencies representing manufacturers of automotive products had eagerly used NASCAR as a promotional tool. Marketing campaigns from the 1950s are responsible for the saying: "Win on Sunday; Sell on Monday." For example, if a Chevy won a major NASCAR event on the weekend, sales of Chevrolets went up for the following week.

Automobile ads in the mid-1950s featured speed. But with rising highway fatalities and the AMA's pull-out from racing, advertising messages backed away from their encouragement of speed.

However, product advertisements continued to make connections between racing and the ordinary consumer. Here are some examples from the 1957 Southern 500 souvenir program:

"Pepsi sets the pace" with an illustration of a young woman holding a cup of Pepsi, with grandstands, race car and pit crew in the background.

In an ill-fated move designed to speed up refueling, fuel tanks were mounted on stands for the 1957 convertible race at Darlington.

For that first Rebel race, the gas tanks were on stands in the pits. Just like at Indy. One caught on fire. Never again. No more elevated fuel tanks in the pits.

—Tom Kirkland

"The 'Pros' bet their lives on their brakes ... and GREY-ROCK BALANCED LININGS provide an extra margin of safety." This ad goes on to say how NASCAR's championship circuit is the "toughest brake laboratory in the world" and how "you" can benefit from using these brakes.

"Champion spark plugs power 136 out of 141 stock car winners! ... This kind of performance shows that Champions are best for your car, too." This ad includes a chart that shows type of track (e.g., short track) and number of wins by manufacturer.

An upscale ad for Plymouth's Fury states: "Heavy-duty, racing-type torsion bars team with new ball-joint construction up front, and new asymmetrical rear springing, for level, no-sway cornering and no-dive, no-dip stops."

Also in 1957, a dress code for crew members was implemented. Shirts had to be worn. NASCAR posted a $100 prize for the "crew making the neatest appearance when lined up for the National Anthem."

The pit area had been "split" in 1956. Half of the cars were assigned pit areas on the front stretch; half on the back stretch. The practice continued in 1957, and it continues today.

By 1957, the Darlington Raceway Network fed its coverage of the Southern 500 to more than 100 radio stations. Announcers "with auto racing reputations" competed for positions on the DRN team. Paul Benson, "general manager of WJMX in Florence, South Carolina, and founder of the racing network," held class to teach correct terminology, pronunciation and racing ethics to selected announcers.

A "local boy" from nearby Timmonsville, South Carolina, made his first Grand National start in the 1957 Southern 500. Cale Yarborough would go on to become a three-time NASCAR champion.

Several have won championships in two consecutive years. To date, Yarborough is NASCAR's only driver with championships in three consecutive years (1976, 1977, and 1978).

Camping Out on the Infield

According to Darlington track records, the infield was opened for camping in 1956. Eager fans were encouraged to get to the track early and stay there. Track management hoped this would relieve some race-day traffic congestion. In 1957, the infield was full of campers.

Traffic was still bad.

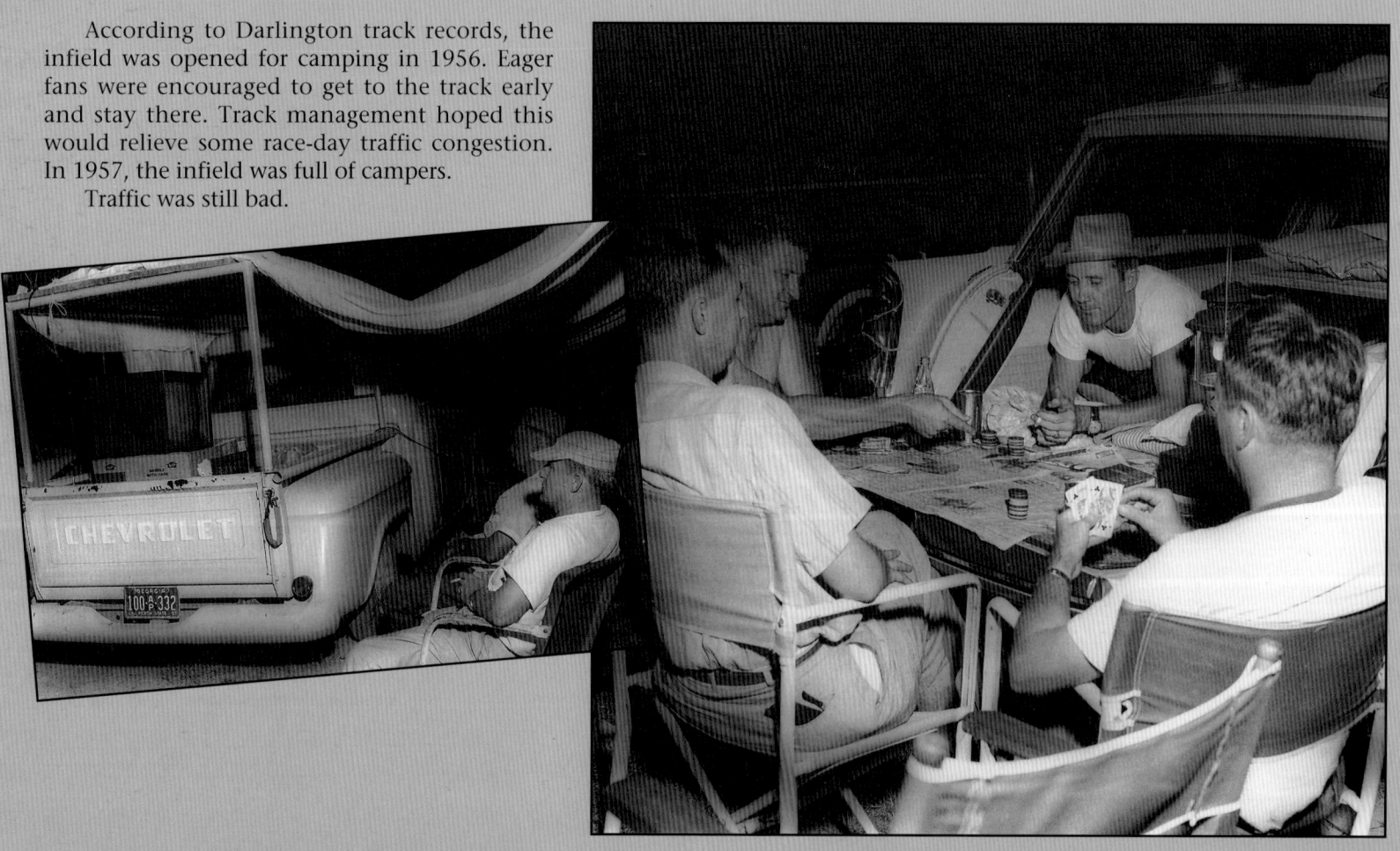

A Most Confusing Situation

This may be the most confusing situation I've encountered in racing. In 1957, Lee Petty was not able to qualify his car for the Southern 500. Lee Petty had Bobby Myers qualify his car (42).

Bobby Myers also qualified his own car, No. 4.

And Paul Goldsmith (3) had Curtis Turner (31) qualify his car. Both were driving cars owned by Smokey Yunick.

This was the year that Herb Thomas came to Darlington, but he was nervous for some reason. He had the shakes so bad that he couldn't drive. Herb had Fonty Flock drive his car in the race.

Curtis Turner qualified for the front row in third position (No. 31). Cotton Owens was the fastest qualifier, and Bobby Myers qualified Lee Petty's car in second.

In this 1957 race, there was a pile-up right at the end of the back stretch. Fonty Flock, who was driving the Herb Thomas car, spun out. It was a black car. When he stopped, the front of his car was facing the oncoming cars.

Fonty had had problems with the car. He had only completed 18 laps when this happened. Bobby Myers and Paul Goldsmith had completed 27 laps.

When Fonty spun out, Bobby Myers (4) was coming down the back stretch with Paul Goldsmith (3) right behind him. Bobby Myers was looking into his rearview mirror at Paul Goldsmith and ran head-on at full speed into the stalled car of Fonty Flock, which had Herb Thomas' name painted on it.

The engine of the No. 4 car that Bobby was driving came out of the car and rolled down the track.

Paul was hurt; Fonty was hurt badly. Bobby was killed.

Chocolate Myers, who is now the gas man for Dale Earnhardt, is Bobby's son.

This front-row picture was made after time trials. Bobby was killed the following Monday in that race.

Something must have told Herb Thomas not to drive that car in that race.

The car Fonty drove was black; the track was black. After that wreck, NASCAR outlawed black cars. I'm not sure when black cars were allowed again, but they outlawed black cars for several years. You could not drive a black car.

—*Tom Kirkland*

Bobby Myers (left) and Cotton Owens.

Paul Goldsmith and Smokey Yunick.

George Parrish spins his 1956 Studebaker in the sandy soil of South Carolina's Pee Dee region.

The Herb Thomas car, driven by Fonty Flock, had spun. It was struck head-on at full speed by Bobby Myers' car. Paul Goldsmith was involved also. Bobby Myers was killed in this wreck. Paul and Fonty were injured.

> *This is what was left of the Herb Thomas car, which was driven by Fonty Flock in this race.*
>
> *I took this photo after the car had been brought back to the pits.*
>
> *This car had spun and was facing the oncoming cars. That's how the head-on collision occurred.*
>
> *Bobby Myers never saw him. He was looking in his rear view mirror at Paul Goldsmith, who was about to pass Bobby going into Turn Three.*
>
> —Tom Kirkland

Speedy Thompson won the 1957 Southern 500 on four tires. Reportedly, he never changed a tire and averaged 100.094 miles per hour.

The race was marred by the death of Bobby Myers in a crash with Fonty Flock and Paul Goldsmith. Also, Joe Caspolich, a Grand National newcomer, was badly injured in a crash on lap 67.

Lee Petty put Curtis Turner into the wall during a battle for position. Joe Weatherly, Turner's housemate, ran down Petty and wrecked him. Turner's car was repaired in the pits by Smokey Yunick and his crew. Turner finished in 11th position.

Thompson collected $13,590 for the win, his 14th career victory.

1958

Chapter 11
Into the Limelight

For the last time, Darlington Raceway would be known as the only superspeedway for stock car racing. Nine years after the first Southern 500, Daytona International Speedway would hold its first events, in February 1959, featuring the Daytona 500.

The timing was perfect. The NASCAR organization had established itself as a reputable sanctioning body. NASCAR drivers had proven they were tough competitors who put on a good show for their fans. Stock car racing was said to have stolen away some of pro football's fan base. And a new, bigger track with higher banking in the turns was scheduled to open in Daytona, NASCAR's hometown.

It was time for NASCAR racing to hit the mainstream.

At the crash-filled 1958 Southern 500, Darlington track photographer Tom Kirkland took four photographs that played a prominent role in bringing stock car racing to the masses. Those photos were the first stock car racing pictures featured in *Sports Illustrated* magazine ("Safe Drivers All," Pages 28–29, September 15, 1958).

Prior to this, print coverage of stock car racing in the national media was limited. Local newspapers in towns with race tracks ran stories about weekend races. A few racing and automotive performance magazines existed, but their circulation was limited to racing fans and automotive enthusiasts. Stock car racing simply was not considered a major, mainstream sport.

Prior to that issue, *Sports Illustrated* had featured sports car racing. It stands to reason. The motorsports editor, John Bentley, was a sports car driver. Many of the events covered by the magazine were races in which the automotive editor participated.

Before Tom Kirkland's work was published, *Sports Illustrated* had printed only one other photo of stock car racing, a small photo of "jalopies" racing around an abandoned polo ground on the East Coast.

A convertible race had been run on May 10, 1958. On the front row for the Rebel 300: Fireball Roberts (right), Marvin Panch (center), and Cotton Owens.

Holman and Moody, shown with an immaculately prepared Thunderbird with Curtis Turner at the wheel, played key roles in NASCAR. Owned by Ralph Moody (left) and John Holman (right), the team has featured some of the most prestigious drivers in the sport. Formed when the two men bought out the Ford racing team's stock of race cars and parts when the factory team lost funding in 1957, Holman and Moody were mainstay builders in NASCAR through to the 1990s. For 1958, they campaigned two cars with Turner and Joe Weatherly at the wheel.

When racing teams wanted to run a new car, they brought it to the track for NASCAR's approval before they could race it.

—*Tom Kirkland*

In September 1958, Sports Illustrated ran four of my pictures on a double page. That was the first time stock car racing was featured in Sports Illustrated.

Kenneth Rudeen, a writer with Sports Illustrated, came to Darlington and told Russ Catlin that he wanted to write a story about the race and he'd like to pick up a picture to illustrate his story. Russ put him in touch with me. He asked how soon after the race he could get a picture. I told him that my darkroom was right there. I would process film right after the race, and I could make him a quick print.

After the race I processed the film and while the film was still in the wash, he came by, and I took it out and just strung out the 35-millimeter film.

I said, "Do you see anything you like?"

Well, he ended up buying 40 prints to take back to New York. And from the 40, they used four.

One of them was the picture of Eddie Pagan hitting the wall in 1958. There was no time for a second picture. The car hit the rail—Bam! And it was gone out of the track. In fact, I didn't even see the car. I never saw the wreck. I shot the picture by impulse. I heard the car, threw the camera up to the sound and clicked.

—Tom Kirkland

Eddie Pagan crashes his Ford through the guardrail during the 1958 Southern 500. Pagan, who qualified on the pole by default (see sidebar), was not injured in the accident.

One of Kirkland's best-known photos was included in the magazine's two-page spread. Eddie Pagan hit the guardrail in Turn One and went right through the guardrail. Kirkland says he never saw the wreck.

"I shot the picture by impulse," Kirkland says. "I heard the car, threw the camera up to the sound and clicked."

Kirkland was using a new camera that day that was capable of taking pictures in rapid succession. This recent innovation in photographic technology allowed a photographer to capture a "sequence" of shots.

The Eddie Pagan crash happened too quickly to get a second shot, even with this new equipment, Kirkland says. Other sequences were captured, however. Some of them are shown in this chapter.

This is highly significant in the history of stock car racing photography. Kirkland was the first stock car racing photographer to capture sequence shots. The days of the single shot were over. (See Introduction.)

His camera was an East German-made Praktina FX, a 35-millimeter camera. The film was advanced automatically with a spring-wound mechanism.

Despite his innovative camera equipment, Kirkland used a primitive darkroom at the track. It was a metal shed. The intense heat affected the "behavior" of chemicals used for developing photos. This forced Kirkland to guess at the time needed to process his photos.

Kirkland says, "If a film had a normal development time of 10 minutes, that was cut down to about 2 1/2 minutes at 100 degrees."

Another indication of the growing popularity of stock car racing was the participation of a celebrity guest in the Southern 500 Festival. In 1958, James Arness was the special guest. Arness played Marshal Matt Dillon on TV's popular show *Gunsmoke*.

The track itself earned a degree of celebrity status. Because Darlington Raceway was the first superspeedway paved with black asphalt, it was called "The Lady in Black." And the asymmetrical shape of the track made the turns difficult to maneuver. So Darlington Raceway came to be known as the track "Too Tough to Tame."

The famous "Darlington Stripe" was earned, particularly in the 1950s and 1960s, when drivers scraped the guardrail in Turns Three and Four. Paint from the cars was left on the guardrail. Motorsports journalists have called that the "rainbow of courage."

Race cars went so fast down the back straightaway that the tail end of the car slid out and scraped along the guardrail after entering Turn Three.

Rex White scored 28 wins in his NASCAR Grand National career (1956-1964). His best year was 1960, when he won 6 times and had 25 top-five finishes. That consistency earned him the 1960 Grand National championship.

Below
Curtis Turner (26) and Joe Weatherly were teammates in 1958. "Atlanta International Raceway" was painted on the sides of their cars. They were promoting the new track at Atlanta two years before it opened.

According to Jim Hunter's *A History of the Darlington Raceway* (1967), "The car bounces off the rail and the driver eases back on the throttle. Before he comes off Turn Four and down the main straightaway, he might have touched the guardrail two, three, maybe four times, or more.'

A young man named Richard Petty registered for the 1958 Southern 500, but he is not listed in the race results. The souvenir program, however, took the opportunity to play up the father and son angle.

Lee Petty, Richard's father, had won the NASCAR Grand National championship in 1954. Lee Petty finished 19th in the 1958 Southern 500. He would go on to win the 1958 championship.

That's a scary situation. Fire. The car actually streamed gasoline behind it all the way across the track. It started burning back on the track and followed the car right until it caught up to it. That's Don Kinberling's car (60) on fire. This was on the seventh lap.
—Tom Kirkland

Joe Weatherly (12), Eddie Pagan (45), Fireball Roberts (22), Joe Eubanks (6), Curtis Turner (26) run three-wide through the turn. Joe Eubanks has what looks like a "6" on his door but a "9" on his roof. He seems to have painted the number on his roof upside down. NASCAR officials require drivers to display a number legible from the infield, as every driver except Joe has done.

Everything happened right between the Turn One and Turn Two.
One, two, three cars went out of the track.
Jack Smith didn't go through the guardrail. He jumped it. The guard rail was still there.
But Eddie Pagan and Eddie Gray both took down guard rails.
There were big holes in the guardrail up there, and they didn't fix them! The race went right on.

—Tom Kirkland

Right: Eddie Gray (8) makes an early exit on lap 160 of the 1958 Southern 500.

I shot one picture of the Jesse James Taylor incident (No. 9) with the 4x5 Speed Graphic, put it down, then started shooting pictures with the sequence camera.

—Tom Kirkland

> *Nothing can be more satisfying than winning at Darlington. You have to drive every second of every lap. There's no time, not even a second, to relax.*
>
> —Fireball Roberts

Right
Bob Colvin grins in the background as Curtis Turner poses with the driver's and mechanic's trophies after the 1958 Rebel 300 on May 10.

Left and pages 80 and 81
Jack Smith (No. 47) jumped the rail in Turn One after completing 210 laps of the Southern 500. After shooting the sequence of the crash, Tom Kirkland crossed the track and shot one more photo—where the car came to rest.

Victory lane at the 1958 Southern 500 (September 1). Cannonball Baker, NASCAR's commissioner, talks with Doris Roberts while a reporter interviews her husband, Fireball.

Eddie Pagan's Pole Position

Here's your front row for the 1958 Southern 500. Eddie Pagan called that his "double breasted" Ford. He put those spinners on there and called it his double-breasted Ford.

Let me tell you how he got on the pole for that race. This'll tell you how they qualified back then.

They held qualifying on two days. The fastest driver on the first day of qualifying got the pole. They would qualify a certain number of cars on the first day. I don't remember how many. The drivers who qualified on the second day started where the first day left off. So, if 30 drivers qualified on the first day, the fastest second-day qualifier started in 31st position for the race. If the overall fastest car qualified

Eddie Pagan and his Ford after qualifying. The ground is wet from a hail storm.

Eddie Pagan (right), Fireball Roberts (center), and Joe Weatherly (left), the front row for the 1958 Southern 500

on the second day, it was possible that the fastest qualifier would not have the pole position.

The track would be open for practice from about 1:00 p.m. until about 5:00 p.m. A car could go out any time during that practice period to qualify.

The way a driver would tell the NASCAR officials he wanted to qualify was to drive his car up to the start-finish line and stop. They would throw the red flag, get all the cars off the track, and let the driver go out and run his four qualifying laps.

After that, if there's another car in line to qualify they let him qualify. Once all the cars that wanted to qualify had qualified, they would re-open the track for practice.

In 1958, the first day of qualifying, nobody went out to qualify. They were practicing.

Eddie Pagan was going out to practice, but he stopped at the start-finish line to adjust his goggles or something. So NASCAR threw the red flag and brought everybody in.

Eddie said, "Oh, I didn't want to qualify. All I was stopped for ..."

They said, "No, you were stopped there. You've got to qualify."

So he started his qualifying laps. During his four qualifying laps, a black cloud descended over Darlington. It started to hail.

Eddie Pagan took the checkered flag, and it hailed for a good 15 minutes. And that was the end of qualifying for that day.

He was the only one to qualify. Therefore, he was on the pole.

And his famous quote was, "Oh, my goodness! Now I got it and don't know what to do with it."

That's how Eddie Pagan got on the pole in 1958. By default!

—*Tom Kirkland*

1959

Chapter 12
Hard Drivin'

During the 1959 Rebel 300, a dramatic "duel at Darlington" was played out by Buck Baker and Curtis Turner. Lap after lap, Turner prevented Baker from passing. Spectators were treated to bumper banging and nose-to-tail action. Baker finished 26th and Turner was scored in 28th. Such intense competition sometimes costs drivers track position. Baker and Turner ended their duel with a spin-out.

Although NASCAR would eliminate its Convertible Division after the 1959 season, the Rebel races at Darlington would be run by "ragtops" until 1963.

The Southern 500 celebrated its 9th anniversary and the 10th race in 1959. Improvements continued to be made to the track's facilities.

The grandstands on the front straightaway were completely covered now. Shady, but loud. The aluminum roof amplified the roar of the race cars. Grandstands had been constructed on the back stretch. They remained uncovered.

Ticket prices for the covered grandstand were $10 each. For seats on the uncovered back stretch, tickets were $8 and $6.

In an article about the 10th running of the race, Russ Catlin, Darlington Raceway's public relations director, wrote: "Since the first Southern 500 in 1950, no one but a Southerner has been able to win the biggest of all." That article was published before the 1959 Southern 500.

Long before the movie *Days of Thunder* was filmed in conjunction with the Daytona 500, *Thunder in Carolina* (later renamed *Hard Drivin'*) was filmed at Darlington Raceway. Rory Calhoun and Alan Hale Jr. starred in the movie.

Scenes for the movie were filmed before, during, and after the Southern 500.

In 1959, the Darlington Raceway Network included more than 200 radio stations located in 26 states. The sport and its media coverage continued to grow.

Fireball Roberts won the 1959 Rebel 300 in a 1959 Chevrolet, defeating Joe Weatherly, who was driving a Thunderbird, even though the T-Birds had been heavily favored. Roberts set a new record for the race with a speed of 115.903 miles per hour.

Movie star Rory Calhoun relaxes in an ambulance at the 1959 Southern 500. Calhoun starred in *Thunder in Carolina*, a movie about stock car racing that was filmed at Darlington Raceway.

NASCAR promoted its "racing family" image with photos taken in 1959 at Darlington Raceway. Four father and son teams participated in the Southern 500: Lee Petty and son Richard; Buck Baker and son Buddy; Shorty Johns and son Bobby; Roy Burdick, and son Bob.

Lee Petty, Richard Petty, Buck Baker and Buddy Baker were all drivers. Shorty Johns (Poppa) and Roy Burdick 'wrenched' for their sons, who were drivers.

NASCAR also promoted a special Baker-Petty "clash" to be held at Hillsboro, North Carolina, on September 20. For this 10-lap, four-car dash, the fathers would start in the second row. The sons would flip a coin for pole position.

Richard Petty led seven laps of the 10th annual Southern 500 and appeared in track records with a fourth-place finish. He was relieved by Marvin Panch, who completed the race. Buddy Baker finished 40th.

More than 78,000 spectators attended the race. First place paid $17,250. The winner was Jim Reed—a Yankee.

As the saying goes: There's a first time for everything.

Buck Baker (87) catches up to Curtis Turner (41)

The Duel at Darlington

Lap after lap after lap, fans watched this 1959 drama play itself out. One car clearly superior to the other; both drivers fighting for position.

This seven-shot series, 6 of which were taken on consecutive laps, embodies one interpretation of the symbolic meaning of racing.

This is stock car racing's equivalent of rutting season. Horns locked in combat until, finally, one is turned away.

Fans know this is the kind of tension and release that built the sport of stock car racing. This is not "parity." This is the struggle of the underdog, the beta male, the working stiff. This is blue-collar America trying on the white collar.

Face your foes, show your stuff, and fight for your position. Not just on the track but in life.

Heroes are born here.

Kids—both young and old—leave the track with a renewed sense of purpose. An understanding of what it means to be "on track." Look inside the cars. Drive and determination.

That's one thing we can see in battles such as this between Curtis Turner and Buck Baker.

One lap later, Turner (41) prevents Baker (87) from making the pass.

Baker (87) tries the low side another lap later, but Turner (41) has him blocked.

The 1959 Rebel 300 marked the first time two cars really had a duel at Darlington. No. 87, Buck Baker, is trying to get around 41, Curtis Turner. And 41 is blocking him.

This is not a sequence. I shot each frame on a different lap.

Finally, they tangled.

We could tell there was a little animosity between Curtis Turner and Buck Baker.

When Buck would go low on the track, Turner would come down in front of him. If Buck went high, so did Curtis.

They raced all over the track then. They didn't have a "groove." They raced wherever there wasn't another car.

The sun was coming out and going in. I had to adjust my shutter speed. It was easy to underexpose the film. The film back then didn't have the latitude it has today.

—Tom Kirkland

Notice the body language. Tension builds with each lap.

Turner (41) still refuses to yield the position to Baker (87). On the eighth lap of the battle, Baker (87) pushes too hard; both he and Turner (41) spin.

Turner (41) still refuses to yield the position to Baker (87).

Jim Reed (7) drives past Turner's spinning car (41).

Lee Petty and son, Richard.

> There were four sets of fathers and sons at the race in 1959: Richard and Lee Petty; Buck and Buddy Baker; Shorty Johns, mechanic, and Bobby Johns, driver; and Bob Burdick, driver, and Roy Burdick, mechanic.
>
> Russ Catlin wanted me to get pictures of the father and son, father and son, father and son, father and son. That's how these pictures came about.
>
> —Tom Kirkland

Buck Baker and son, Buddy.

Cotton Owens . . . and a mechanic's leg.

Cotton Owens preferred racing on dirt tracks. The South Carolina native started 160 NASCAR races between 1950 and 1964, and recorded 9 wins and 18 second-place finishes.

His best finishes at Darlington included second place in the 1957 Southern 500 and a fifth-place finish in the 1962 Rebel 300.

Richard Petty had raced for the first time in a convertible race on the dirt track at Columbia, South Carolina, on July 12, 1958.

The 1959 Southern 500 was the first superspeedway race of his career. Richard Petty was credited with a fourth-place finish, although he was relieved by Marvin Panch.

Banjo Matthews would come in 10th in championship points for the 1960 season. But he is best known as a car builder.

His best finishes at Darlington Raceway were seventh place in the 1960 Southern 500 and eighth in the 1961 Rebel 300.

Speedy Thompson (22), Fireball Roberts (3), Elmo Langley (10), Richard Petty (43), Banjo Matthews (93), Rex White (4), Joe Weatherly (12), Lee Petty (42), a car obscured by a photographer, Bob Welborn (49), and Bob Burdick (73) charge through Turn One on the first lap of the 1959 Southern 500. Note the helicopter, which happened to be in the frame.

This photo represents my days as a car owner. I was a part-owner of this car, driven by Joe Caspolich.

This was the same car Lee Petty drove when he won Daytona in 1959, the inaugural race there. Lee had signed a contract with Chrysler to drive Plymouths, but they had not gotten all of the parts and everything he needed to him in time for the Daytona race. He had been running Oldsmobiles. So he built this Oldsmobile for Daytona. It ran that one race. He won the race and sold the car.

We bought the car, just like it was when it finished the race, with one spare engine and 16 wheels with tires mounted. In those days, the same tire was used for all tracks. We paid $5,000 for the whole thing.

Several of us went in on this car ownership deal. There was Red Tyler (who would become vice president of Darlington Raceway in 1967), Allen Windham, Scrunt Schipman, Joe Caspolich, and me. Each of us put up $1,000.

Joe got his money together by going to all the people he had met in town. He spent about two months in the hospital in Florence, my hometown, after a wreck.

Joe went to the doctors, nurses and everybody else he could find and asked them for money . . . $25, $50, or $100 . . . whatever he could get. That's how he came up with $1,000.

The car was known as the Paperhanger's Special. We borrowed that name from a car that had raced in Indianapolis years before. It was owned by hundreds of people. The co-owners would put in $100 or $200 . . . whatever they could afford.

They couldn't figure out what to call the car.

Well, they had a doctor, a lawyer, a minister, a photographer, a banker, and a surgeon. Every profession—except a paperhanger. None of the co-owners hung wallpaper for a living. So they called it the Paperhanger's Special.

Joe Caspolich and the *Paperhanger's Special: City of Florence*. The car finished 13th in the 1959 Southern 500—not well enough to earn a profit for its co-owners.

Like these folks in Indianapolis, we had doctors, lawyers, a photographer, and so forth in on the sponsorship. I don't think we had a minister. So we called that car the Paperhanger's Special, the City of Florence.

It didn't do too well. It finished in 13th place. Prize money for 13th was only $470.

We didn't meet our expenses.

The car ran a couple of the races after Darlington and never did well. At the end of the season, we sold it.

—*Tom Kirkland*

The front row for the 1959 Southern 500: Fireball Roberts on the pole, Elmo Langley (center) and Speedy Thompson on the outside. Elmo Langley may be best known as the pace car driver for NASCAR's Winston Cup Series. He died in 1996 while in Japan for the inaugural Suzuka Thunder Special 100, NASCAR's first race in the Orient. Note the barefoot boys inspecting Speedy Thompson's ride.

Left: Johnson's Southern 500 run ended early in a horrific crash during practice that ripped the engine right out of his car.

Jim Reed (7)—a Yankee!—arrives in victory lane after winning the 10th annual Southern 500. A veteran of short track racing, Reed led 152 of the 364 laps. This was Reed's first experience leading a race at a superspeedway.

1960

Chapter 13
The Lady in Black Strikes

Both races at Darlington Raceway, the Rebel 300 and the Southern 500, were successful at drawing big crowds and attracting the best drivers. Eldridge Thompson, a reporter for the *Charleston News & Courier* newspaper, attributed the success of the track to the people who ran it. The directors and staff of Darlington were ordinary hard-working citizens.

'There isn't a man on the staff who isn't as plain as an old shoe," Thompson wrote. "There's color, sure, but the actual event provides it, not the prepublicity and hoodwinking that goes on at many other tracks."

One member of the staff was track announcer Ray Melton. He had been recruited by Darlington Raceway officials, who had been listening to race track announcers across the South.

Melton's job began a few days before time trials began. He visited the garage area, talked to drivers and mechanics, and gathered other information he could use during those long hours on the public address system.

According to Melton, qualifying provided the greatest challenge. Time trials were held over an extended period of time. If no one chose to qualify, that left large gaps that needed to be filled by the announcer.

Some announcers played records during such lulls. But not Melton. He interviewed drivers, mechanics, and track officials.

During the race, Melton watched for signals from the drivers. Some telegraphed their moves on the track with their mannerisms. Melton says Joe Weatherly gave him a nod or a wave that would indicate his next maneuver. Melton watched for it and reported it through his microphone.

Most sports writers were not privy to such hand signals, however. Bob Talbert, a sports writer for the *State* newspaper in Columbia, South Carolina, described the biggest challenge of covering stock car racing: Unpredictability.

"Just when you've dreamed up a flowery lead for a story, a tire blows and seven cars pile into each other," Talbert said.

To counter skeptics who refused to believe stock car racing was a sport, Talbert said: "A stock car driver is an athlete, make no mistake about that. He has the strength of a boxer; the skill of a golfer; the reflexes of a shortstop; the quickness and agility of a basketball guard; the stamina of a swimmer; the mind of a quarterback; and the heart of a distance runner."

According to Talbert, racing fans demanded complete coverage in their newspapers. They were knowledgeable about their sport and they expected accurate, thorough coverage. Talbert described stock car racing fans as "the most avid fans in the world.

At first, every race car that came to the track underwent a technical inspection. The heads were taken off. The cubic inch was determined. NASCAR has always had strict rules.

Everything was torn down on all cars.

They figured out that this took too much time, so the NASCAR officials said, "Okay, fellas. We're going to tear down certain cars. So you'd better be legal. Everybody had better be legal."

A cursory inspection was done on all cars. But random cars—or those that won too often—had to go through a tear-down, in which parts of the motors were taken out for close inspection.

—Tom Kirkland

In the interest of fair play and of putting on a good show for racing fans, NASCAR periodically "tore down" cars that finished in top positions. NASCAR rules mandate a maximum lift height for a cam. Higher lift allows more air to enter the cylinders, which causes greater compression and a more powerful explosion of gas and air in the cylinders. That translates into more power. A cam has been mounted on a lathe for inspection.

The Miss Southern 500 beauty pageant was held the Saturday night before Monday's race. A runway was set up on the track at the start-finish line. A panel of judges, seated at the table on the right, scores each contestant. The trombone player's sheet music is titled "Boogie."

They will travel 500 miles during a weekend, sleep in a car, and eat little, just to see a race. They want and deserve their news. Darlington makes fans, and fans make racing."

In 1960, as always, there was plenty to watch. Top speeds on the straightaways exceeded 120 miles per hour.

Building cars that would go that fast required special talent and skill. Some of those who built race cars were becoming as famous as the drivers.

Smokey Yunick was one of the first mechanics involved with NASCAR to develop "star" status. He was known for his technical innovations, and famous for bending the rules.

Yunick's innovations in the pits helped turn the five-minute pit stops of the early 1950s into the 18-second pit stops of the 1990s. Something as simple as carefully organizing tools in the pits eliminated frantic searching for tools during a pit stop.

Bud Moore of Spartanburg, South Carolina, had developed a reputation for building cars "sturdy enough to finish and fast enough to win." Jim Foster, sports editor for the *Spartanburg Herald* reported Moore's response to a rival who teased Moore about failing to qualify fastest.

Moore said, "So what? It's not how fast you start but how fast you finish."

As of 1960, Moore had built cars for Joe Eubanks, Jack Smith, Buck Baker, Speedy Thompson, and others.

Lee Petty also appreciated the hard work it took to prepare a car that would finish a race. Humpy Wheeler, then a sportswriter for the *Columbia Record*, reported Lee Petty's formula for success: "When a fellow wins a race or finishes among the leaders, you know somebody has been working hard. Three-fourths of a race is won in the garage. The best driver in the world can't win if his car doesn't hold up."

Smokey Yunick was said to have worked an entire year to prepare a single car for one particular race.

Darlington's Pure Record Club was established in 1960. Inducted into the club was the fastest qualifier for each make of car entered in the Southern 500.

Charter members were the top qualifiers from 1959's Southern 500: Speedy Thompson, Chevrolet; Elmo Langley, Buick; Dick Joslyn, Dodge; Marvin Panch, Ford; Richard Petty, Plymouth; Fireball Roberts, Pontiac; Bob Burdick, Thunderbird; and Joe Caspolich, Oldsmobile.

Members of the club were to form a committee "to instruct and approve rookie drivers for the Southern 500."

Members served as official spokesmen at all events related to the Southern 500. A ring, an emblemed dinner jacket, stationery, and driving suits were awarded to new members. The induction ceremony was held during an annual banquet at the VFW Club in Florence.

Prize money for the Southern 500 increased over the years. The total purse in 1950 was $25,000. By 1960, it was $90,000.

The 1960 Southern 500 featured a terrific battle between Buck Baker, Fireball Roberts, and Richard Petty. However, the race was marred by tragedy. Bobby Johns wrecked in Turn Two, sending the car down pit road. Johns was not seriously injured, but three people working in the pits were killed.

The race was won by Buck Baker, who became known as "The Old Pro."

Joe Caspolich drove the 1960 Rebel 300 with his foot in a cast. He finished in 12th position.

On lap 95, Bobby Johns and Roy Tyner made contact in Turn Two. This sent Bobby Johns spinning into the backstretch pit lane. Mechanics Paul McDuffie, Charles Sweatlund, and NASCAR official Joe Taylor were killed in the accident. Bobby Johns was not seriously injured.

They are attending to one of the pit crew members. Paul McDuffie's sombrero is in the foreground.

> *You acquire the taste of stock car racing when you've been around it for a while. You learn to shut the door on the tragedy which is lurking always on the other side. You educate yourself as the drivers do... as people who face up to life... to think about the good things and sip only the sweet wine of life.*
>
> *You realize the world of stock car racing is often cruel, demanding, punishing, sickening, a masculine sport of many things. But you think about the good side, as men in all phases of life are so prone to do....*
>
> *You watch the real professionals in action, admire their skill and their courage, and hope none of the sincere rookies fighting for a chance make an unforgivable mistake....*
>
> *You wonder for a moment but the door closes on the tragedy that is always something of a freakish nature and the wine of life that pours itself on the world of stock car racing tastes sweet once again, and the good things seem closer than before.*
>
> —Wylie Carolina, 1967 Rebel 400 Souvenir Program

In this sequence, Carl Burris (9) spins while Bob Welborn (49) ducks under him in a close call. Bunkie Blackburn (64) isn't so fortunate, and he spins and crashes into Burris. Burris and Blackburn were each paid $200 in winnings for their efforts in the 1960 Rebel 300. Burris finished 26th, one position behind Blackburn.

Johnny Allen's car came to rest near the fence to the parking lot after taking a bite out of the scorers' stand in the 1960 Rebel 300.

We saw Johnny Allen's car go off the track in Turn Three and down the embankment. We didn't see anything again until we saw the scorers' stand crumple.

This was during the race, so the scorers were up there.

Fortunately, the sun was shining into the end that the car hit. So, all the scorers who had been in that section had moved down to the shady end. No one was sitting right where the scorers' stand crumpled. And no one was hurt. Johnny Allen walked away.

The scorers had to get down by ladder because the steps were mangled by the car.

There was one lady who just would not come down the ladder. Somebody had to go up and bring her down. She just would not come down that ladder.

—*Tom Kirkland*

Pre-race festivities for the fourth annual Rebel 300 featured St. John's (Darlington) High School band.

The 1960 Rebel 300 was eight days long. The race began on May 7. But rain began to fall on lap 58. After 74 laps had been completed, the race was stopped. The race resumed a week later, on May 14.

NASCAR declared that the race would begin under caution. Joe Weatherly had pitted under the yellow flag on May 7. Other leaders had not stopped. Weatherly argued that the yellow flag restart stripped him of his strategic advantage. NASCAR officials refused to give in. But Bob Colvin, Darlington Raceway's president, assured Weatherly that Colvin would drive the pace car for the restart. They were to be the fastest pace laps ever run.

The controversy over the restart was good for ticket sales. On May 7, 25,000 fans were in attendance. For the restart on May 14, 37,000 fans were in the stands.

Buck Baker won the 1960 Southern 500, driving Jack Smith's No. 47 car. Owner-driver Jack Smith won 21 races in his 15-year NASCAR Grand National career.

The pit crew for Fireball Roberts' car, owned by Smokey Yunick (left). For the time period, this is an uncommonly well-organized NASCAR pit space. Everything is laid out in an orderly manner for easy access. This helped assure efficient pit stops during the race. The tire behind Smokey is painted with "LF Set 2." The four tires in Set 1 are mounted on the race car for the beginning of the race. Set 2 will probably go onto the car during the first pit stop. "LF" indicates "left front." Within the same set, tire pressures and tire diameters are varied or "staggered" to improve handling.

Joe Weatherly, winner of the rain-delayed 1960 Rebel 300. His "Rebel 300" shirt is a souvenir item that was sold at the track. The price in 1960: $4.

1961

Chapter 14
Pomp and Circumstance

Before a stock car race begins, tension builds. Activity increases. Then, there is a moment of silence before the thunder of racing engines shudders through the grandstands.

Russ Catlin, Darlington Raceway's public relations director, outlined the pre-race ritual:
- Wednesday before the race: Time trials begin.
- Thursday and Friday: "The tempo increases, the speed, the competition and partying. The town is highly decorated and everywhere the Confederate motif prevails."
- Saturday: Festival day, complete with parade, aerial shows, military bands, the Miss Southern 500 beauty pageant, dances, and celebrity appearances.
- Sunday afternoon: The infield gates open and a "rural Mardi Gras" begins. Music and laughter fill the air.
- Race day: Two hours of pomp and ceremony. Then a prayer and a salute to the flag before a Southern voice says, "Gentlemen, start your engines."

Although factory involvement came and went, most of NASCAR's racing teams relied on homemade innovations. As in the earliest days of racing, performance improvements were made largely by independent mechanics working in service stations or home garages.

To honor this tradition of creative problem solving, the Independent Garage Owners of America (IGO) presented mechanics of winning cars with a trophy. The IGO believed that "stock car racing has evolved from the ideas and efforts of mechanics in independent garages over the country."

When auto manufacturers realized that stock car tracks were excellent "proving grounds," it was IGO mechanics who were called upon to set up those race cars. "Performance on the race track sets the pace for the cars that will be on the highways tomorrow."

Safe automobiles on safe highways was a goal of the Champion Highway Safety Program, sponsored by the Champion Spark Plug Company.

Champion hired professional race car drivers to tour high schools across the country, where they stressed the importance of safe driving. These tours were cosponsored by a local automotive parts wholesaler and the Champion Spark Plug Company.

Freddie Agobashian, a veteran driver at Indianapolis and Darlington, said: "We stress our code of safety [sic] driving, namely: (1) mental alertness, (2) courtesy and (3) good mechanical condition of the car." Agobashian believed that this program helped "young drivers, the drivers of tomorrow, save their lives and the lives of others."

One of Darlington's favorite drivers, Joe Weatherly (Little Joe) wore a scar on his face from a highway accident. On the track, Weatherly drove "flat out," but on the streets and highways, he was known as a "legal-limit driver."

He had won an American Motorcycle Association championship before World War II, and then made the switch to four-wheeled racing machines.

According to Bob Talbert, feature writer for the *State* newspaper in Columbia, South Carolina, Weatherly was "a Huckleberry Finn in a crash helmet." Weatherly was humorous, serious, and generous, and he spoke up "for all the other drivers' rights against wrong or misguided rules and regulations." Known for his antics at the track, Weatherly was referred to as the Clown Prince of Racing. He was a practical joker.

The mongoose box was his best known and most effective prank. According to Bud Moore (in Peter Golenbock's book, *American Zoom*), Weatherly had a box with a wire mesh over it. He told people that inside the box was a fast, ferocious exotic animal from China called a mongoose. People would get close to the box to get a look at this creature. When they got very close

This picture was taken with an in-car camera. But this was not during practice or in a race. Tom Kirkland wanted a photo of what a driver sees on the track. So Kirkland climbed aboard Curtis Turner's Ford convertible. He was lying across the back of the car to get the proper angle for this shot. Tom Kirkland had asked Turner to take it easy. The car headed into the turn at about 60 miles per hour. For Curtis Turner, that is taking it easy. Tom was hanging on for dear life!

to the box, Weatherly would push a button and a fox tail would spring out of the box and brush against them.

The people were scared. Weatherly laughed. There was no mongoose.

Away from the track, Weatherly was famous for his parties. He was a gentle man who carried a club. A Canadian Club.

According to Bob Talbert, Joe Weatherly was a winning driver with a colorful personality who made money for people. In 1961, he had a bright future as a driver and as a spokesperson for racing-related products.

One new racing-related product came to Darlington in 1961. The Peach State Scoreboard Company introduced Darlington Raceway to the "Scorebrain." This was an electrically engineered scoreboard that displayed, in lights, the car number and number of laps completed for the first five positions.

The Scorebrain was wired to a control panel in the track's scoring booth. The control panel used a telephone dial to enter car numbers. A push button was used to add to the lap count. And a second telephone dial was used to correct the lap count, if necessary. A scorer in the booth entered race data by hand. by pushing the button or dialing.

However, a two-page ad announcing the new scoreboard exaggerated the abilities of this device: "The Scorebrain functions as a highly developed electro-mechanical controlled system that can actually think, reason and perform features which are normally associated with complex electronic computers and guidance systems for aircraft."

David Pearson climbs from his car. Pearson had won Rookie of the Year honors in 1960. A fierce competitor, Pearson won 102 races in 574 starts, and was NASCAR's Grand National Division champion in 1966, 1968, and 1969.

Emanuel Zervakis (left), Jim Reed (center) and Ned Jarrett (right). Emanuel Zervakis was called the "Golden Greek." He started 83 races and won two. Between 1956 and 1963, he raced in NASCAR's Grand National Division. To save film, Tom Kirkland called the three drivers together. Kirkland later cut out the drivers' heads for use as mug shots in souvenir programs.

Fireball Roberts (right) held the pole position for the 1961 Southern 500. Fred Lorenzen was on the outside of row one. By 1961, the front row had been reduced to two cars rather than three. The cars were fast enough that they needed a little more "elbow room" getting through the first turn.

Roscoe Thompson (24) spins during the 1961 Southern 500.

Roscoe Thompson (24) continues to spin, as David Pearson (3) looks for room to pass near the rail.

Thompson's (24) car moves down the track, and Pearson (3) aims for the opening.

Pearson (3) has missed the spinning car of Thompson (24). Now, T.C. Hunt (10) watches the No. 24 car as he passes on the low side of the track.

The Smokey Ban

Banned from the pits in 1961, Smokey Yunick was forced to sneak in and hide. When asked about this photo, Yunick said, "I don't remember ever being banned from the pits. But if I was, I wouldn't have paid any attention."

Smokey Yunick was always challenging the NASCAR officials. He was caught with illegal parts on his cars relatively often. And Smokey is not known for his tact.

For some reason, Smokey Yunick was banned from the pits during the 1961 Southern 500. He was not allowed to act as crew chief for his own car. And he was not allowed to be on pit road during the race.

But he snuck back in and hid behind a building to keep an eye on things.

I saw him and got this picture of him hiding from the NASCAR officials.

—Tom Kirkland

Nelson Stacy caused motorsports journalists to do some quick homework. Little was known about Stacy before the 1961 Southern 500. He had entered one NASCAR race in 1952. He won his second NASCAR race, the 1961 Southern 500. He came back to win the 1962 Rebel 300. He scored 7th in the 1962 Southern 500, 4th in the 1963 Southern 500, and 39th in the 1964 Southern 500. He left NASCAR racing in 1965. Reportedly, Stacy was a quiet, intellectual, honest man who never used profanity and had a hearty appetite. His handshake was described as bone-crushing. The quiet Nelson Stacy disappeared when he strapped himself into his race car. According to the 1962 souvenir program, Stacy's "eruption comes in a race. On the track he is noted as liking it rough." Miss Southern 500, Mary Ann Brunnemer, is wearing two pins, both military emblems. The 1961 race honored "Fifty Years of Naval Aviation."

Right
Nelson Stacy rolls his 1961 Ford into victory lane. He took home $18,430 for winning the 12th annual Southern 500.

1962

Chapter 15
Johnson . . . er, Frank

In 1962, just as it is today, stock car race fans were infatuated with personalities.

Tony Webner, racing director for Goodyear Tire and Rubber Company said: "The interest of spectators isn't just for speed alone, but for the competition between drivers and cars. The fans have favorite personalities and car preferences, and they cheer for that hero, or particular make of car, to win."

In the stands, the infield, or in the radio audience, fans cheered for their favorites.

Radio coverage of stock car racing from Darlington was broadcast worldwide by 1962. WJMX in Florence was the Darlington Raceway Network originating station. Paul Benson, Jr., manager and coowner of WJMX, is credited with establishing the network of almost 300 stations, including a feed to the Armed Services Network.

According to Sadie B. Wantin in the 1962 Southern 500 program, Benson described the network's audience: "The fans listen for the race itself, not for accidents. Among the most rabid of the fans are women—old women, young women, shut-ins, all kinds."

By 1962, Benson arranged for a representative from the U.S. Weather Bureau to be on hand to talk about the weather. Today, NASCAR has its own portable "weather station" for monitoring race conditions.

The Darlington Raceway Network eventually would be sold to a NASCAR-owned enterprise known as the Motor Racing Network (MRN).

Among favored drivers was "the bachelor of the circuit," Fred Lorenzen (Fearless Freddy). Handsome, blond and single, Lorenzen was particularly popular among the fan base Benson had referred to as "rabid"—women of all kinds.

According to Marcus Holland, sports editor of the *Savannah Morning News*, Lorenzen was "racing's champion of clean living."

Holland said, "Always first at the track, Fred, a carpenter and mechanic by trade, rarely smokes and never drinks anything other than water, milk and cherry pop."

Lorenzen joined NASCAR in 1960. In 1961, he was signed by John Holman and Ralph Moody as Joe Weatherly's replacement.

"From the moment Lorenzen entered big league racing, he was tabbed as a future Fireball Roberts or Joe Weatherly," Holland said.

Before the 1961 Rebel 300, people had noticed Lorenzen as he practiced.

"With the courage of a champion and the vim of a young rookie, the 'barn walker' (high-strung horse who blows off steam by walking in his stall) lifted a few eyebrows as he became stronger and better with each lap," Holland said.

Lorenzen set a qualifying record: 128.965.

Ned Jarrett (Gentleman Ned) had won his first Grand National championship in 1961. He was another crowd favorite. His wife, Martha, and his children, Glenn, Dale, and Patty, were among his biggest fans.

Jarrett told Bill Kiser, sports editor of the *Concord Tribune*, "If you're running for the championship, you have to change your philosophy. You have to change your style. You must finish the races. Many times I wanted to charge, to go all out to win, but I had to settle for a position farther back. It's not easy to do."

Jarrett had bought his first race car for $100 from a friend who owed a gambling debt.

Jarrett is described as "modest and unassuming but as energetic as a colony of ants at a picnic." His energies were devoted to his family, stock car racing, his lumber company, his franchise for survival kits, and his record company.

Jarrett's Speedway label cut a record called *Go or Blow*. The author obtained a scratchy old recording of the song from a racing fan in Columbia, South Carolina.

The fan bought the record from Jarrett in 1962. Jarrett was selling records from the trunk of his car at Columbia Speedway. Not all the lyrics could be deciphered. Here is what the author heard (words in brackets are best guesses):

Fred Lorenzen (28), Ned Jarrett (11), and Tom Pistone (82) run three-wide through Turn One in the 1962 Southern 500.

In the 1962 Southern 500, Red Foote's (84) attempt at three-wide racing results in a spin. Sherman Utsman (61) and Emanuel Zervakis (20) continue racing. An "unmanned" ABC-TV camera can be seen in the upper left, near the guardrail.

Red Foote (84) continues to spin as Elmo Langley (82) takes the high side.

Behind Pistone's (82) car, Jack Smith (47) had spun to avoid Foote's (84) car. Smith comes to rest in the infield, out of the race in lap 111. Foote recovers and continues racing.

Go or Blow

Men were rough an' tough on the [?] trail, they were brave at the Alamo. But in the old South land, There's a breed of man the racing fans all know.

From track to track, to hell and back, they're racing day and night. The fans gather 'round when the motors sound. They're gonna go or blow tonight.

(Refrain) There's a long track waiting at Darlington, Daytona and Charlotte town. Qualify on Saturday night, before the sun goes down.

So pick up all [your paces boys] Even though she looks [real tight] We'll run 'er flat out And [never give up ground] Until she blows tonight. *(end of Refrain)*

Just buckle yourself in the driver's seat, you're sitting on the pole. Every heart stops when the green flag drops. Tonight you're going to roll.

With a mighty flash, Ol' Ned goes past. Little Rex is a' hangin' tight. You're gonna take this purse, or a long, black hearse. You're gonna Go or Blow tonight.

(Refrain)

You're on it again, down the long back stretch. You're right up next to the rail, while Fireball ace is neck and neck, with Junior on your tail.

Ned Jarrett leads at the halfway mark, but you're still hangin' tight. Then the oil she throws, as the motor blows. You'll make the long haul home tonight.

(Refrain)

Another popular racer was selected to receive a "father of the year" award in 1962.

In its second year of giving this award, Gabriel Shock Absorbers asked the Southern Motorsports Press Association (SMPA) to select Gabriel's Racing Father of the Year. Lee Petty was named.

The SMPA said: "Those of us who saw the Richard Petty of today start out a few years ago well remember the attention, encouragement, and years of knowledge passed from father to son in the early days. His devotion to his wife and family, his tireless efforts to fight the good fight through many years of active participation in our sport certainly qualifies Lee Petty as the "father of the year," and may more of us look to him as an example of what kind of father we should be."

Larry Frank was a family man, too. But he was not that famous until he won the 1962 Southern 500 . . . hours after the race.

Junior Johnson had been flagged for the win. But a scoring error had been made. (It could not have been the Scorebrain's fault, could it?)

The day after the race, Tom Kirkland was asked to return to the track to photograph the true winner. Kirkland already had photographed Junior Johnson in victory lane.

After shooting pictures of Larry Frank, Darlington Raceway asked Kirkland to show Frank in victory lane with Miss Southern 500. Kirkland took that photo the day after the race. The Darlington PR Department cut Frank's face and pasted it onto the shoulders of Johnson.

The result was a little out of proportion. Larry Frank was much smaller than Junior Johnson. But the composite photo was used for promotional material, anyway.

According to Wilt Browning, sports writer for the *Greenville News*, Larry Frank was obsessed with racing.

Frank said: "When I'm not racing, I sometimes get really hard to get along with around the house. But then if I can get on a track somewhere and run a little bit, I'm all right again."

Frank had had trouble securing a good ride. He felt that the scoring error at Darlington hurt his chances. Interviewed in 1963, Frank talked about that.

"If I had been in victory lane," he said, "Ford would have gotten full benefit out of it and it is possible I would have been set for a ride all this season [1963]. But the fans went away thinking that Junior Johnson and Pontiac had won the race."

That was not the only problem at Darlington Raceway in 1962. According to Russ Catlin, Darlington Raceway's public relations director, Joe Weatherly refused to sign an entry blank that had the number 13 on it. He would not register until the race was renamed the "Twelfth Renewal."

In addition to photographers and reporters, NASCAR and Darlington Raceway arranged to have a documentary film crew on hand for the events.

According to Chuck Johnson, president of Victory Films, Inc., "A good documentary racing film should supply authentic details of the general situation and outcome of the race itself and should tell the complete story with action interestingly portrayed through a series of closely knit scenes. Movie making should begin where still pictures leave off."

Eleven camera operators filmed the racing action. Film crews shot pre-race footage, as well. Because not all drivers could be covered, documentary filmmakers concentrated on the Top 10 contenders.

According to Johnson, these drivers were "always available to assist you in any way they could—taking you out in their expensive [sic] built cars for special effects shots, posing for publicity shots, or just hamming it up for the cameraman. You don't get this kind of cooperation from the Hollywood stars."

Sponsors of the race viewed the film. Some scenes were of particular interest to certain companies. For example, "In the

On lap 275 of the 1962 Southern 500, Johnny Allen's Pontiac (46) hit the guardrail and punctured the fuel tank. The car burst into flames. Allen climbed from the car, uninjured.

Members of the Gaston Speedway First Aid Crew, Gaston Life Saving & First Aid Crew, and Darlington Rescue Squad extinguished the flames. Some of the firefighters are wearing asbestos suits.

With the race under caution, Rex White (4) can be seen passing the smoldering remains of Allen's car. This was the second fire during this race. On lap 186, Darel Dieringer's Ford had crashed and burned.

H.G. Rosier (5) spins just in front of Cale Yarborough (92) during the 1962 Southern 500. At more than 100 miles per hour, Yarborough knows one thing: Either he will hit the No. 5 car, or he will miss it. There is no time to steer clear of the spinning car.

Yarborough lifts his foot off the gas pedal and waits—rolling along at high speed. Rosier sees Yarborough's car and, stomps his gas pedal to the floor (right), "smokes" his tires to escape a collision with Yarborough.

Yarborough holds his line, Rosier clears the track, and Yarborough races past without a scratch.

1960 Southern 500 film, no less than six drivers either spun-out or wrecked right in front of the Falstaff [beer] sign at which we had a camera position," Johnson said. "We haven't been able to find out if this was loyalty to a sponsor or wishful thinking on a real hot day. In any case, this made Falstaff happy."

In the fall of 1962, Darlington Raceway announced the hiring of Lester Becker as a movie producer for Darlington Films, Inc. He had directed the Southern 500 documentaries from 1955 to 1958. These films had won "best documentary" awards at the Brussels World Fair, Edinburgh (Scotland) Film Festival and the Columbus, Ohio, Film Festival.

Becker said, "I am most pleased when the mechanics and drivers say, 'I learned a lot about the race from watching that film of yours.'"

Pure Oil had been the official gasoline of Darlington Raceway since 1951. George Brain supervised Pure Oil Company's crew at the track. He was honored by Darlington Raceway for his 10 years of service to racing.

Bob Colvin, president of Darlington Raceway, said: "We owe more than we can ever give to George Brain and Pure. They are to us like grits are to ham and eggs."

The Petty family (from left): Richard; Linda, Richard's wife; Lee; Elizabeth, Lee's wife; Maurice's wife; and Maurice, Richard's brother. The clock Lee is holding was for being awarded "Stock Car Racing's Father of the Year" for 1962 by the Gabriel Company.

Left
Junior Johnson, his wife, Flossie, and Miss Sun Fun USA, Ginger Pointevint, celebrate in victory lane. Although Johnson was credited with the win that day, NASCAR officials later discovered a scoring error. The next day, Larry Frank was announced as the real winner of the 1962 Southern 500.

Below
Larry Frank is presented his trophy.

After the fact, Larry Frank was named the winner of the 1962 Southern 500. Old Larry was a ne'er-do-well. Never really finished well. And all of a sudden he wins the Southern 500!

And NASCAR didn't give it to him. They said Junior Johnson had won the race. Well, the win was awarded to Larry Frank the next day.

Frank knew he had won the race.

Russ Catlin had me come back to the track and shoot some photos of Frank. You can see that the grandstands are empty in this photo.

They took those pictures of Johnson in victory lane and put Frank's face on them. Out of proportion.

They used those pictures of Larry Frank's head on Johnson's body for publicity the following year.

—Tom Kirkland

Darlington claims Cale Yarborough as its hometown hero of stock car racing. Yarborough is from Timmonsville, South Carolina, just a few miles from Darlington. Active in South Carolina politics, Yarborough's 385-horsepower Ford displays campaign messages. The bumper sticker near Cale's arm says: "McNair for Lt. Governor." The small poster near the front tire says: "Compare with care—vote McNair, Lt. Governor."

1963

Chapter 16

"Little Rebs" and Big "Tiny"

The 1962 Rebel 300 had been the last convertible race at Darlington. The 1963 Rebel 300 was run by hardtops.

Reportedly hoping to attract a crowd accustomed to seeing convertibles race in the spring, Bob Colvin instituted a format change for the 1963 Rebel 300. The format was adopted from a race held in Monza, Italy, and modified for Darlington.

Rather than one 300-mile race, two 150-mile races called "Little Rebs" were run.

The first Little Reb had a conventional running start, with starting positions earned by qualifying time trials.

After 150 miles, the checkered flag was thrown.

A mandatory 30-minute break was taken by the entire field, during which repairs could be made without penalty.

Bob Colvin assured fans this break in the action was a continuation of the race: "The mechanic is working against the clock, and his skill and ability will either aid or hinder his driver."

The cars were required to return to the track within 25 minutes.

To start the second Little Reb, drivers lined up in finishing order of the first race. This Little Reb began from a standing start.

One fuel stop per race was expected. So speedy performance in the pits was critical.

Any car that dropped out of the first race could return at any time.

Bob Colvin said, "The car having traveled the farthest and the fastest in the combined Little Rebs would be declared the winner of the Rebel 300."

Colvin encouraged fans to write to the track after the race. "Tell us what you liked or did not like about the race. To us, the public is the boss, and your wishes will be given every consideration." This Monza-style format seems similar to today's format for NASCAR's truck series and its no-points race at Charlotte, "The Winston."

Cale Yarborough wears a short-sleeved flight suit to drive the 1963 Southern 500. Stock window glass is still in the race car. Note the two metal braces bolted over the rear window. The cars went fast enough at this point to blow out the back glass without such supports.

Clint Eastwood was 1963's celebrity guest at the 14th annual Southern 500. Representing the television show *Rawhide* in Darlington, Eastwood was known for his character Ramrod Rowdy Yates. He was "Honorary Chief Steward" for the race. He helped judge the Miss Southern 500 beauty contest and served as grand marshal for the Southern Festival downtown parade.

Two big men participated in the 1963 Southern 500. Each stood at 6 feet 4 inches.

The first was a 275-pound fish camp owner who raced stock cars. His name was Tiny Lund.

Lund struggled to find good rides for a while. He persevered, and his wife, Ruthie, showed great patience. Racing is a family business.

Lund said: "Me and Ruthie would go wherever there was a race. She would talk about me giving up racing every once in a while when things were going bad, but she would never have made more than a suggestion. She never pressed the issue, and I never gave up."

The second big man was Honorary Chief Steward Clint Eastwood. At the time, Eastwood starred in TV's *Rawhide* series as Ramrod Rowdy Yates.

In addition to his race day role, Eastwood also helped to judge the Miss Southern 500 beauty contest and served as grand marshal for the Southern Festival parade through downtown Darlington.

The 1963 Southern 500 was won by Fireball Roberts. This would be Roberts' last victory at Darlington Raceway.

1

2

3

1. Hardtops ran the Rebel 300 race in 1963. The convertible division had been eliminated. During that race, Fireball Roberts (22) loses traction and tangles with Bobby Johns (7A).

2. Look inside the cars. Feel Fireball Roberts grip the steering wheel as he fights to keep control of his race car.

3. Both drivers calmly correct for the skid.

4. Roberts is out of the skid completely, while Johns is still fighting to straighten out.

5. Both Roberts and Johns recover and continue racing. Bob James (27) can be seen near the rail, about to pass Johns, who is getting back up to speed.

Linda Vaughan, Miss Firebird, rode this float—a big product logo for Pure Oil's Firebird Gasoline mounted on a trailer. Unlike a Miss Southern 500 beauty queen, Vaughan was a professional marketing representative. She was hired by the Pure Oil Company to promote its products. Linda Vaughan's face—and body—are famous in NASCAR circles. Vaughan had become a racing beauty queen at age 14, and became the first professional sex symbol associated with professional stock car racing.

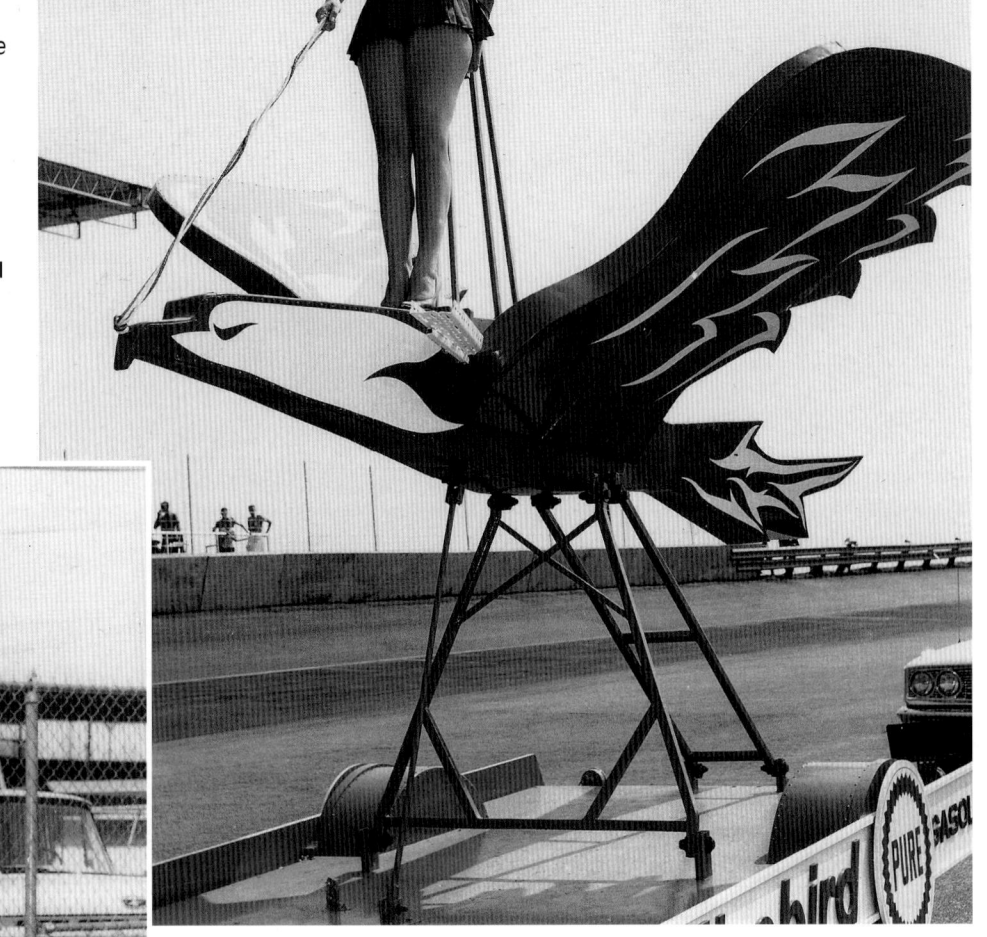

Drivers would often joke around before a race. In '63, one of the pre-race promotional gimmicks was a burro race. The drivers were supposed to ride burros and race them down the front stretch to entertain the crowd.
Tiny Lund was not tiny, not by any stretch of the imagination. He said, "I'm too big for this little burro. I'd better carry it." So he picked it up. These guys had a lot of fun with each other at the track.
—Tom Kirkland

Johnny Reb

"Johnny Reb" rides the Fireball Roberts car into victory lane after the 1963 Southern 400 (September 2).

The Johnny Reb character was a creation of Darlington Raceway. Johnny Reb received credit in each souvenir program, beginning in 1961. Jimmy Patterson, of WBT radio in Charlotte, North Carolina, was the first Johnny Reb.

From 1962 to 1967 (the last year covered by this book), Bob van Witzenburg served as Johnny Reb. He worked at WJMX.

Under the direction of Paul Benson, WJMX radio in Florence, South Carolina, had created the Darlington Raceway Radio Network.

By the mid-1960s, this network broadcast races live from Darlington Raceway to 35 states—from Massachusetts to California and Montana to Florida.

The Darlington Raceway Radio Network would evolve into what has become the Motor Racing Network (MRN).

Darlington Raceway created a character called "Johnny Reb." A fellow was hired to dress up as Johnny Reb and carry the Confederate flag around. He's in pictures of victory lane. And he was there for photo opportunities with special people—celebrities and politicians and so forth.

Oddly enough, he was not a Southerner; he wasn't a Yankee, either. He came from Holland!

Bob van Witzenburg was an exchange student from Holland who went to high school in Charlotte, North Carolina. When he finished high school, he got an extension to stay in the United States, and he went on to college.

He ended up in Florence, South Carolina, working for WJMX radio. This station owned the racing network at that time.

—Tom Kirkland

1964

Chapter 17
No More Monza

The 1964 Rebel 300 program was dedicated to Joe Weatherly. He had been fatally injured in a non-collision racing accident at Riverside, California, on January 19, 1964. He was 41 years old.

Weatherly had won both split-race Rebel 300s: the one in 1960 interrupted by rain and the intentionally split format of the 1963 race.

The Monza-type format adopted for the 1963 Rebel race—with its two Little Rebs separated by a 30-minute intermission, during which mechanics rushed to make adjustments and repairs to their cars—did not last.

The original Monza format called for a timed event. Whoever went the farthest the fastest won. But NASCAR officials chose to run a race based on positions rather than distance.

It was discovered a few days before the race, however, that NASCAR scoring system could result in multiple ties from first to last. So officials decided to award points for positions in each race.

This would eliminate the possibility of ties and should eliminate confusion over the scoring system. So they thought.

Bob Colvin had told fans they were the boss. He wanted their feedback about the split-race format. And he got it.

Fans were confused by this format.

And the frequent threat of rain caused anxiety among drivers, who wondered how NASCAR would interpret the rules. For example, if a rain storm began during the intermission, who would win?

So fans and the weather caused race officials to change the format for the 1964 Rebel race to a straight 300-mile event with a rolling start.

Fred Lorenzen was awarded $10,265 for winning the 1964 Rebel 300.

Fireball Roberts had a fiery crash during the World 600 in Charlotte on May 24, 1964. Roberts died from complications on July 2. Roberts was the second of NASCAR's top drivers to lose his life in 1964 because of a racing mishap.

Fireball Roberts had competed in every Southern 500. He had won two of them, and he had six other Top 10 finishes. He had earned five pole positions for the Labor Day race. Roberts had won two Rebel 300 races and had four other Top 10 finishes in the Spring race. He started the Rebel race twice from the pole.

Bob Cooper's 1963 Ford (53) drives past the spinning 1963 Dodge of Major Melton (36). An unidentifiable car crashes into Melton's car, while Richard Petty's 1964 Plymouth (43) speeds past what may be the first billboard visible from the Darlington Raceway grandstands. In 1959, many drivers had arrived at the track driving their race cars. By 1963, open trailers—many of which appear to have been homemade—carried stock cars to the races. After "dropping" the car off its trailer and unloading tools, drivers parked the trailers at one end of the infield, away from the pits.

Cale Yarborough prepares for the 1964 Southern 500. He is wearing a "cool suit." The cool suit is designed to circulate water through the driver's fire-resistant uniform. Dual exhaust pipes run directly beneath the floorboard of the car, and in-car temperatures easily exceed 120 degrees Fahrenheit. The windshield wiper mount has not been removed from the car. It can be seen at the base of the windshield.

Pat Hanna (reprinted in the Southern 500 program from a July 11, 1964 article in *Motor Classics*) referred to Fireball Roberts as "The King of Speed."

However, by the mid-1960s, Fireball Roberts was being eclipsed. In 1964, Richard Petty began emerging as a favorite. He would come to be known simply as "The King."

Buck Baker won the 1964 Southern 500. At the time, he was 45 years old and a grandfather. Jim Paschal finished second. Baker and Paschal were the only two drivers to have competed in every stock car race at Darlington Raceway "during the 15-year operational span of the nation's oldest major stock car arena," Russ Catlin said.

Only one sports writer had predicted Buck Baker would win. According to Russ Catlin, the newspaper reporter had said, "Buck Baker is a threat every time he goes to the post at Darlington, even if he is driving a wheelbarrow!"

But he was not driving a wheelbarrow. The winning car was a 1964 Dodge with a Hemi motor. NASCAR later decided that the Hemi gave Chryslers an unfair advantage. It was "too fast." By the 1965 racing season, the Hemi would be outlawed.

Lee Roy Yarbrough had won the Daytona 250-mile Modified-Sportsman race twice, but he had not won at Darlington. He would finish 17th in the 1964 Southern 500. In his NASCAR career, which ended in 1972, Yarbrough posted 14 wins in 198 races. His best year was 1969, when he won the Daytona 500, World 600 at Charlotte, and the Southern 500 at Darlington.

David Pearson and Richard Petty get together for a moment before the 1964 Southern 500. The door handle is still on Pearson's' car, although the push button that would open the latch has been removed. A piece of sheet metal has been pop-riveted onto the handle where the button had been. Sheet metal has also been pop-riveted to the interior of Pearson's car to cover sharp edges and conceal how much of the door frame and other skeletal steel has been cut out to lighten the car. A minimum total weight for the car is specified by NASCAR rules. And a maximum percentage of that weight can be left-side weight. Too much weight on the left side of the car would give it an unfair advantage in negotiating the turns at high speed. Race car fabricators are allowed to redistribute weight for proper balance.

A Tragic Loss

Stock car racing lost one of its great drivers when Fireball Roberts died in May 1964. This photograph of him was made at the 1958 Southern 500.

Fireball Roberts' last win was at Darlington Raceway. He set a record with an average speed of 129.784 miles per hour. to take the checkered flag in the 1963 Southern 500.

According to Russ Catlin, beginning about six weeks before Roberts' death, he had talked at length about his racing experiences. Ordinarily, Roberts was quiet about his accomplishments. During this time, he made an hour-long tape on which he told his racing stories. The tape was used as an audio exhibit at the Joe Weatherly Stock Car Museum at Darlington.

He had just signed a lifetime personal appearance contract with Falstaff.

Roberts began his Darlington career in the inaugural Southern 500 in 1950. He started 67th and finished 2nd. He beat the legendary Red Byron, who came in 3rd. When Byron retired, he passed along the number 22 to Roberts.

Roberts won the first Rebel 300, in 1957. Other major races he won at Darlington include the 1958 Southern 500, the 1959 Rebel 300, and the 1963 Southern 500.

In addition, Roberts won the Modified-Sportsman race at Darlington on July 4, 1954. Other notable finishes include: fifth place, 1951 Southern 500; eighth place, 1952 Grand National race in May; third place, Modified-Sportsman race on July 4, 1952; seventh place, 1954 Southern 500; fifth place, 1958 Rebel 300; seventh place, 1959 Southern 500; ninth, 1960 Southern 500; fifth, 1961 Rebel 300; second, 1961 Southern 500; second, 1963 Rebel 300; and second, 1964 Rebel 300.

This picture was made for Gabriel shock absorbers. Fireball Roberts was really on top of the sport for a while. Until the fire.

Fireball Roberts died in a fiery crash during a race at Charlotte, North Carolina, May 24, 1964. I was there.

I wasn't working for the newspaper or the track. I was just doing freelance photography. But I was right there on the back stretch. Right where he ended up.

If I'd had a fire extinguisher, he probably would be alive today. If I had had a fire extinguisher, I could have put that fire out.

Afterwards, I recommended to NASCAR that they require two things: That every person who got press credentials, every photographer who was out around the track, would be proficient in the use of a fire extinguisher; and that fire extinguishers would be placed at given intervals all around the track. So that a photographer would be no further than 100 feet from a fire extinguisher at any time.

They didn't do it. NASCAR didn't do it.

—Tom Kirkland

Bobby Johns (7) misses the "kiss" between the No. 16 of Darel Dieringer and the No. 26 of Bobby Isaac. This action took place during the 1964 Southern 500.

Darel Dieringer (16) creates a cloud of tire smoke as Bobby Isaac (26) pushes him out of the way. Paul Goldsmith (25) avoids the incident by diving to the inside of the track.

Bobby Isaac (26) speeds past as Darel Dieringer (16) slides toward the infield.

Elmo Langley (64) appears to be close to Tom Kirkland's vantage point as Darel Dieringer (16) hits the sandy infield.

Junior Johnson displays his new Darlington Pure Record Club ring. The ring has the Pure Oil logo next to a checkered flag. The words "Darlington Pure Record Club" are engraved on it. In 1964, Junior Johnson was inducted into the Darlington Pure Record Club, which had been formed in 1960. Each year, the fastest qualifier for each make of car was inducted. Other 1964 inductees included: David Pearson, Dodge; Bobby Johns, Pontiac; Neil Castles (Soapy), Chrysler; and G.C. Spencer, Plymouth.

Top Mechanics

A winning effort is always a combination of a driver's talent, racing luck, and the hard work of mechanics and other crew members. Houston A. Lawing listed top mechanics of the time in the 1964 Rebel 300 program (in no particular order):

John Holman
Ralph Moody
Herb Nab
Wayne Mills
Jack Sullivan
Gene Beithelete
John Wanderer
Henry Yunick (Smokey)
Ray Fox
Ray Nichels
Louis and Crawford Clement
Bill Stroppe
Bud Moore
Glen and Leonard Wood
G.C. Spencer
Herman Beam
Larry Frank
Ken Myler (Red)
Roy Osborne
Bondy Long
Bobby Schuyler
Cotton Owens
Pops Eargle

Elzie Wylie "Buck" Baker (second from left), winner of the 1964 Southern 500, accepts congratulations from his son, Elzie Wylie "Buddy" Baker Jr. Sherri Sellers, Miss Southern 500, reigns over the victory lane celebration.

1965

Chapter 18
Little Joe's Legacy

The Joe Weatherly Stock Car Museum, located at Darlington Raceway, opened May 2, 1965. Joe Weatherly had died at Riverside a little over a year earlier.

According to Russ Catlin, Darlington's public relations director, the museum was Weatherly's idea. He had wanted to recover some racing relics thought to be lost, such as the Modified Plymouth with which he had won the 1953 national Modified championship. The car was still racing in the Florida keys.

Before his tragic crash in May 1964, Fireball Roberts served as advisor for the museum project. Ground-breaking ceremonies took place in November 1964. Curtis Turner, Weatherly's teammate and friend, turned the first spade. The museum building was located just behind the original concrete grandstands.

Because of a mild winter, construction of the building with its 6,000 square feet of floor space progressed well ahead of schedule. The raceway board set the opening date for May 2, 1965. But, Catlin said a million-dollar hail storm and spring tornado severely damaged the almost-completed building, and construction had to start all over again. The May 2 opening date was still the goal; the Rebel 300 would be held on May 8.

The museum opened on time and was open to the public. Admission was free. The museum was closed only on Christmas and Labor Day. The museum was not open during Southern 500 races because of the large crowds, and cars on display were removed to be driven around the track for a parade lap.

Past and present drivers made audio tapes to by played through "the perpetual Muzak music program." The drivers described, firsthand, their racing experiences. The tape made by Fireball Roberts ran nearly an hour.

Aside from auto manufacturers, other corporate sponsors were represented as well. Firestone presented a history of racing rubber at Darlington. Pure Oil provided an educational display that explained the functions of racing fuels. And Grey-Rock, manufacturer of brake parts, provided an interactive exhibit, a brake machine that visitors could operate.

Another interactive display was a simulator. According to Catlin, Pure Oil had a display in which a visitor could "sit in a racing bucket seat, grip a racing wheel, look down the main

Car owner Bud Moore (second from left) presents to Bob Colvin (center) the key to a restored Mercury, last driven by Joe Weatherly. Moore provided the car as a display for the Joe Weatherly Stock Car Museum.

Stock Car Exhibits

About a dozen historic race cars were installed as exhibits at the Joe Weatherly Stock Car Museum. Among those were:

- The 1963 Ford Fireball Roberts drove to victory in the 1963 Southern 500; restored by Holman and Moody and donated by Ford Motor Company.

- Buck Baker's 1950 Plymouth, first entry in the first Southern 500; sponsored by Griffin Motors in Florence, South Carolina.

- A 1950 Plymouth representing the one that won the first Southern 500, a hybrid with "enough parts from the original to establish a relationship" with the replica, restored by Hubert Westmoreland.

- The 1957 Chevrolet built by the late Paul McDuffie and driven to victory by Fireball Roberts in the 1957 Rebel 300.

- A 1962 Pontiac that earned two Daytona wins with Fireball Roberts at the wheel.

- Jim Reed's 1959 Chevrolet from the 1959 Southern 500, actually, a replica built to original specifications.

stretch of Darlington Raceway and feed gasoline into a motor by operating an accelerator. Gauges register such items as rpm and power boosts."

Twelve trophy cases were filled with awards, trophies and personal effects. Some of Joe Weatherly's personal possessions displayed were his saddle oxford shoes, golf gloves and Darlington shirt, all of which he wore when racing.

On display were racing engines and illegal parts impounded from race cars by NASCAR technical inspectors.

The museum also housed the Southern Motorsports Press Association's Hall of Fame.

Within six months of opening, the museum hosted more than 100,000 visitors.

With Joe Weatherly and Fireball Roberts gone, the track seemed to show its age. But Jim Hunter, sports editor at the *Columbia Record*, described a feisty track, not a decrepit one.

"This is the story of a race track, a rustic old creation of speed that lives on in a quickening world of progress," Hunter said. "It is the story of an outdated arena of excitement where man and machine take the test of life. Darlington Raceway offers a black surface of asphalt with a complexion that changes daily. Its inconsistency in the turns has surprised the bravest of rookies ever to run and has baffled the smartest of pros who have toured its groove more than most people have purred down a rural highway. Only the brave ones wear the Darlington stripe."

Despite its age, experienced drivers returned year after year. The myth of the track grew. Newcomers dreamed of conquering this track. According to Hunter, the Darlington Raceway "demands and gets the respect and admiration of those who come here to seek out its

The blond from the Chicago suburb of Elmhurst, Illinois. A carpenter by trade, Lorenzen began his NASCAR career in the hobby division. He left NASCAR to run USAC late models, and won USAC championships in 1958 and 1959. He returned to NASCAR competition in 1960.

By the fall of 1965, Lorenzen had become the first driver to win major events (not in the same season) at all four of NASCAR's superspeedways—Daytona, Atlanta, Charlotte, and Darlington. He drove Fords for the Holman-Moody team out of Charlotte. He won the 1964 Rebel 300 with an average speed of 130.013 miles per hour. At the time, he was the sport's leading money winner.

Fred Lorenzen was a carpenter from Elmhurst, Illinois, in the Chicago area. He heard about a demolition derby in Chicago. A friend of his had an old car. They put it in the derby, and he won it. He was hooked.

He was quite a popular fellow. Especially with the girls.

Wherever you saw girls, Fred was in the middle of them.

—Tom Kirkland

secrets of prestige and pride, of money and glory, of conquest and victory."

Notable new faces on the Grand National circuit in 1965 included: Wendell Scott (a popular driver who happened to be the only black racer), Dick Hutcherson, Ned Setzer, and Bobby Allison (winner of three championships in NASCAR's Modified Division). Tom Pistone, Doug Yates and a few others returned to the circuit in 1965.

In addition to attracting top drivers and thousands of fans, the events at Darlington Raceway brought new business to South Carolina's Pee Dee region. The Perfection Gear Company—which made stock and performance automobile parts—moved its operation from Chicago to the north side of Darlington in 1965. The company built a 300,000-square-foot plant on 102 acres.

Thunder in Carolina had been filmed at Darlington Raceway in 1959. In 1965, *Red Line 7000*, a movie about "girls in love with race car drivers," was scheduled for release.

Producer Howard Hawks said, "We shot actual races all over the country. In every case, our camera car was a qualifying entry, and it usually finished in the money."

The script was a composite of three stories that had interested Hawks for years.

"Alone, none of the stories would have made a full-length feature," Hawks said. "But by using auto racing as a theme to link them, we have a story that works."

Actual film footage of racing at Darlington was included in the film.

On lap 118 of the 1965 Southern 500, Cale Yarborough was challenging Sam McQuagg for the lead. The cars made contact and Yarborough sailed over the guardrail. He never touched the guardrail. His car literally flew over the barrier.

According to Russ Catlin, documentary films showed that Sam McQuagg "lost the front end in attempting to block an inside charge by Yarborough, kissed the Yarborough metal and the resulting touchoff sent the Yarborough Ford into orbit."

"Yarborough had been giving McQuagg the Vukovich shag," Catlin said. "This is a trick as old as racing itself, in which one driver feints inside another, then outside and so on, never passing, until the front car driver's head swivels like Mortimer Snerd's in looking for the next charge. Past victims, to a man, declare this to be the most brutal of legal trickery."

McQuagg was leading the Southern 500 in an independently backed car.

McQuagg was a carpenter in his hometown of Columbus, Georgia, when he decided to become a stock car driver. He spent his savings on old cars and raced hard in Georgia and Florida for three years, building his reputation as a charger.

His performance as a driver attracted the attention of Mrs. Betty Lilly, "a wealthy sportswoman from his hometown." She bought him a good race car and sponsored his efforts.

By leading the 1965 Southern 500 during laps 88 to 118, he attracted the attention of veteran car builder Ray Nichels. In 1966, McQuagg would have a factory ride in a white Charger fastback.

Neither Yarborough nor McQuagg was injured in their mishap. However, Buren Skeen died nine days after the 1965 Southern 500 from injuries suffered in a crash on the second lap.

According to Greg Fielden's *Forty Years of Stock Car Racing* series, Skeen lost control of his car and Reb Wickersham's Ford "T-boned" Skeen in the driver's door. "Skeen's bucket seat was knocked to the right side of the car," Fielden said. "Rescue workers took nearly 20 minutes to get him out of the car. He never regained consciousness."

Despite safety precautions, stock car racing was—and still is—a high-risk profession.

In victory lane, Festus (Ken Curtis) and "Doc" Adams (Milburn Stone) from the TV show *Gunsmoke* greet Ned Jarrett and Miss Southern 500, Vickie Johnson. Martha Jarrett celebrates her husband's win. Johnny Reb seems pre-occupied. Ned Jarrett would go on to win the 1965 NASCAR Grand National championship.

1. During the 1965 Rebel 300, Darel Dieringer (16) outruns Bobby Johns (7).

2. Johns spins.

3. Doug Cooper (35) tries to evade the incident.

4. Cooper gets caught in a thick blanket of tire smoke.

5. Johns and Cooper go door handle-to-door handle.

6. Then Cooper powers his way past Johns (7).

Cale Yarborough (27) and Sam McQuagg (24) get tied up in the turn.

Darel Dieringer (16) heads low to avoid the accident. Lee Roy Yarbrough (3) is caught on the high side of the track.

Driving a race car is like dancing with a chain saw.

— Cale Yarborough

From *American Zoom* by Peter Golenbock

A crowd gathers for the museum opening. Dressed in their "Sunday best" clothes, two girls (lower left) prefer to remain barefooted.

Cale Yarborough sails toward a spectator parking lot. When Yarborough's car finally hit the ground, it rolled over several times, but Yarborough was not injured. Lee Roy Yarbrough (3) soon makes contact with the No. 24 car as it slides across the track.

1966

Chapter 19

Legends of the Lady in Black

Over time, Darlington Raceway assumed a nearly human character, complete with personality traits and mating behaviors, at least in the minds of motorsports journalists.

Sportswriter Benny Phillips wrote the 1966 version of the annual tribute to Darlington Raceway:

"As treacherous as Mata Hari, as desirable as Hollywood's most beautiful actress, as unpredictable as any woman, these are the virtues of 'The Lady In Black.' Her curves are long and dangerous, and her waistline narrow and hazardous," Phillips said. "Only the bravest of men dare woo her. Her heart is as cold as the frozen North, and she holds no respect nor fear for any man.

"Only twice each year, once in the spring and once in the fall, does she choose a mate."

The Rebel 300 gained 100 miles to become the Rebel 400, and Richard Petty won it—his first race win at Darlington. Junior Johnson, winner of the 1965 Rebel 300, retired from driving but stayed in racing as a team owner.

Also driving during races at Darlington was Barney Wallace. He was not a racer, though. He was Darlington Raceway's vice president and pace car driver. Back then, the pace car was called the "safety car" or "caution car."

Barney Wallace had been associated with Darlington Raceway since the idea for the track was born. Persuaded by Harold Brasington to invest, Wallace was an original stockholder. Wallace had been Darlington Raceway's vice president since shortly after the first Southern 500.

In 1956, Wallace was Darlington Raceway's second-largest stockholder. The track bought him a station wagon. According to the 1966 Rebel 400 program: "The brightly lettered station wagon was a familiar sight at every NASCAR race from Memphis to Middlebury. At most every track, the car was used as the 'safety' car, with Wallace driving, until the politicians got their grubby paws in the act and local celebrities were featured making like race drivers."

NASCAR drivers protested, and insisted that Wallace drive the safety car.

One driver comfortable behind Wallace's caution car was Curtis Turner. According to Dick Thompson, public relations director at Martinsville Speedway, Curtis Turner began racing in 1946 at Mount Airy, North Carolina.

"He took his family car, a maroon-colored Ford sedan, and roared through a rainstorm that turned the dirt track into a river of mud," Thompson said. "Curtis had the fans yelling that day, and admittedly he had previous practice in dodging police road blocks."

In other words, Turner had run some moonshine.

The first NASCAR point standings in 1949 showed Turner in sixth place. "The rest of the men in the top 10 are either retired or dead," Thompson said.

Turner had been Joe Weatherly's teammate.

"We worked together and lived together there for a long time, and we partied together six nights a week," Turner said. "But when we got on the tracks, we forgot about that until the race was over."

Peter Golenbock said in *American Zoom*: "Off the track. Turner loved women, V.O. and 7-Up, and flying. When he threw a party at his 14-acre home, it might last a week. His rule was you had to get drunk. If you didn't, you didn't get invited again."

Turner worked in the timber business, estimating board footage by flying his own plane over stands of timber. He owned movie theaters.

And he founded Charlotte Motor Speedway with Bruton Smith. Before it emerged as a successful enterprise, the track went through tough times.

Turner hoped Teamster boss Jimmy Hoffa would help save the failing track. According to Golenbock, Turner wanted race drivers to earn 40 percent of each purse (winnings were split between driver and car owner). As members of the Teamsters union, drivers could demand that percentage. In return for his

Richard Petty had won his first of seven NASCAR Grand National championships in 1964. "Richard" is painted on the driver's door. By now, everyone knows his last name. Petty holds a shop rag. He would wet the rag and clench it in his teeth during a race. It was his way of keeping dust out of his mouth.

efforts to bring new members to the Teamsters, Turner believed Hoffa would assist the Charlotte track in some way.

But NASCAR's Bill France believed that Turner and Hoffa had a hidden agenda, to introduce pari-mutuel betting to stock car racing. France felt this would ruin the integrity of the sport.

The effort to unionize failed. And Turner was barred from NASCAR competition "for life" in 1961 for attempting to organize race drivers for the Teamsters Union. He was reinstated by NASCAR in 1965.

Cale Yarborough went through some tough times, himself. His early attempts at NASCAR racing were frustrating.

He had returned to farming and semipro football when the 1965 season began. Shortly after that, Ford recruited Yarborough to drive a factory-sponsored car built by Banjo Matthews, who had joined the ranks of famous mechanics. Things went better after that.

It was tough for Yarborough to perform poorly. According to Jim Hunter, sports editor of the Columbia (South Carolina) *Record*, Yarborough was competitive, even as a boy.

Fred Lorenzen with three of his biggest fans.

"He was the kind of boy who not only would jump out of backyard swings as they reached their highest point, but turn a flip on the way down," Hunter said. "If somebody else turned a flip, he'd turn two flips."

Yarborough said, "You try your hardest, drive your heart out, and people say, 'The hell with the also rans'. Those people might be right, but one of these days it's the young guys like me that are gonna be on top. You can't get there driving an old worn-out machine, and it's hard to keep driving and driving without that once in a while feeling you're getting somewhere."

Before the 1966 Rebel 400, Yarborough said, "I'd rather win at Darlington than any other track on the circuit. I saw my first race here and fell in love with the sport. You can't imagine how thrilled I would be if I could win here."

But Yarborough was not listed among the participants in the 1966 Rebel 400.

Another intensely competitive stock car driver was David Pearson.

"I've always wanted to win at Darlington," Pearson said. "I remember that first Southern 500 way back in 1950. I must have been 12 or 13 years old. I would crawl in my dad's car in the driveway and play like I was Johnny Mantz."

Reportedly, Pearson occasionally allowed a boy who showed the right kind of interest to climb into his race car . . . and pretend to be David Pearson.

Pearson had won the South Carolina Sportsman championship in 1959. He raced Darlington for the first time in the 1960 Southern 500. He finished 27th.

Pearson had been named Rookie of the Year in 1960.

In 1966 Pearson drove a Dodge prepared by Cotton Owens in the Southern 500.

Pearson described the challenge of driving at Darlington: "The only way you can win at Darlington is to stay out of trouble and stand on it. If you stand on it, you'll probably find trouble, but that's the chance you take."

Describing his driving approach at Darlington Raceway, Pearson said, "There's only one groove, so you have to plan ahead on each lap. When you get behind a slower car you have to figure how to pass him. For instance, you figure your distance on one lap and then back off up the straightaway so you can get enough speed to pass him coming off the turns."

David Pearson finished third in the 1966 Southern 500. He would go on to win the NASCAR Grand National championship in 1966.

This four-picture series of Earl Balmer (71) during the 1966 Southern 500 presents a challenge in relaying a factual account of Balmer's troubles during the race.

One source (Forty Years of Stock Car Racing, Volume III, Big Bucks and Boycotts, 1965-1971, by Greg Fielden) tells a story of Balmer's accident on lap 189. Balmer is credited with a 30th-place finish, having completed 185 laps (the leaders had completed 4 more laps than Balmer). Apparently, Richard Petty tapped Balmer from behind going into Turn One. Balmer's car climbed the guardrail and appeared to be headed straight into the press boxes.

However, the car caught on the guardrail and was kept on the track. Several guardrail posts were shattered by Balmer's car, and, according to this report, Balmer's fuel tank ruptured. This was said to have sent wood splinters and gasoline into the press box, where reporters ran for cover.

Fielden reports a 28-lap caution period, during which members of the media corps issued a complaint to Bob Colvin, president of the raceway. The complaint demanded a new location for the press box because "the present press box at the track is without equal in racing from a standpoint of peril to human life."

But Tom Kirkland recorded two separate incidents of Earl Balmer riding the rail in the 1966 Southern 500. The numbering on his negatives supports his story.

On frame "5A" of Kirkland's 35-millimeter film, Earl Balmer's (71) Dodge nearly flew into the Press Boxes (far left, 1 of 4). No one in the press box appears to be running for cover, despite the fact that many could see the bottom of Balmer's race car. Kirkland's frame "6A" is shown here as ["2 of 4."] Wooden guardrail posts are flying. Balmer's head has been thrown forward by the force of the crash. Kirkland's frame "7A" is shown here as ["3 of 4."] Balmer's car has landed on the track, but two large chunks of guardrail post can be seen flying.

According to Tom Kirkland—and his negatives—Earl Balmer continued racing after this ride on the guardrail. Perhaps this first incident caused the 28-lap caution period during which the media allegedly protested the location of the press box. Kirkland clicked off another 21 pictures before shooting frame "31A," shown here as "4 of 4."

This second rail-riding incident appears to have been caused by Richard Petty's No. 43 car. The ambulance is positioned in Turn One, past the press box. The ambulance crew does not appear to be alarmed by the sight of Balmer's car climbing the rail. No one is running for cover.

Perhaps this second accident is the one that put Earl Balmer out of the 1966 Southern 500 on lap 189.

Earl Balmer (71) shows the undercarriage of his car to the press during his first of two runs on the guard rail in Turn One during the 1966 Southern 500. Balmer attended the drivers' meeting shown on the previous page—kneeling, wearing sunglasses.

Earl Balmer heads for a rough landing after ripping out several guard rail posts.

Large chunks of guard rail post remain airborne after Balmer's car lands on the track.

Earl Balmer (71) rides the rail for the second time during the 1966 Southern 500. Richard Petty (43) may have hit Balmer from behind, sending him onto the guardrail.

1967

Chapter 20
The End of an Era

The year 1967 marked the end of an era at Darlington Raceway.

Lee Petty and Buck Baker were stepping aside, while their sons took over as NASCAR's rising stars. Fred Lorenzen and Ned Jarrett retired from driving.

Darlington lost one of the men who helped found the track when Bob Colvin, president of Darlington Raceway, died. And 1967 was the last year Tom Kirkland shot pictures of stock car racing at Darlington Raceway.

Bob Colvin died in his office at Darlington Raceway Tuesday, January 24, 1967. At age 47, Colvin suffered a massive heart attack. "Those close to him said he fought it bitterly, that he simply refused to die," Bob Myers of the *Charlotte News*, said. "That was his very nature."

Colvin was known for his bald head (Colvin attributed it to "miles, not age"), cigars, sense of humor, warm hospitality and his dedication to Darlington, South Carolina, and its raceway.

Colvin began driving at age 11. He put himself through college by driving a truck from Florida to New York, hauling produce. He attended Clemson and Auburn universities, and earned a degree in chemistry.

After a stint in the Navy, Colvin passed up a chance to work for a large chemical firm and took over the family's trucking business. His father, who owned a wholesale grocery business, was ill.

"In those days, we used to pull the engines from the trucks," Colvin said, "install them in race cars for a Sunday race at some dirt track, and then put them back in time for work Monday."

Colvin helped raise enough capital to build Darlington Raceway in 1950. Setting the example for the industry, Darlington Raceway inspired construction of other superspeedways: Daytona, Charlotte, Atlanta, and Rockingham.

A jolly but tough diplomat, Colvin served as the unofficial moderator of several of NASCAR's biggest disputes: Chrysler's withdrawal of its cars from competition in 1965; Ford's 1966 boycott of NASCAR racing; and Curtis Turner's suspension in 1961. For the benefit of his track and for the sport of stock car racing, Colvin worked to resolve each of those disputes.

Two days after his death, Darlington paid tribute to the man who had guided Darlington Raceway to its success. Crowds came to Trinity Methodist Church in the heart of Darlington. Five Southern 500 winners were in attendance at the funeral: Buck Baker, Curtis Turner, Larry Frank, Ned Jarrett, and Darel Dieringer.

Myers described the scene: "There near Bob was a flora of the Confederate flag. Outside, the crowd gathered in the streets, this time to watch Bob Colvin run his final lap. The town stood still and bowed its head. A traffic jam developed, reminiscent of Southern 500 day. The checkered flag has fallen for Bob Colvin. His engine simply burned out."

Barney Wallace assumed the duties of president at Darlington Raceway.

A generation of racers and a track administrator had passed. Transition was in the air, including a shift from cheering Buck Baker, the Old Pro, to rooting for his son.

Buck Baker, survivor of the infamous tomato juice crash in 1950, lived to earn his reputation as the "Old Pro" of the NASCAR circuit. He had won championships in 1956 and 1957.

Since 1958, Buck Baker had been mentoring a young driver, his son, Buddy. Buddy Baker began racing in 1958 in a Grand National event in Columbia, South Carolina.

According to a 1960s Columbia Speedway driver, Buddy Baker drove through the fence in Turn One early in the race. Buck Baker reportedly said, "Buddy, if you didn't know where to go, why didn't you just follow the other guys?"

Buddy studied his father's racing techniques and tried to follow in his father's tire tracks.

Interviewed in 1967 by W.W. Cary, Buddy Baker said, "I learned a lot by following him [Buck] in races. I took the corners

Richard Petty sucks on a rag during a pit stop in the 1967 Rebel 400. Petty had qualified second, so he avoided a major pile-up at the start of the race. A rail separates cars from pit crews. A concrete wall separates pit road from the track. In 1950, a white line painted on the asphalt had marked pit lane, and a guardrail had separated the track from the infield.

A sheet of plastic covers Buddy Baker's Dodge (3). Buddy relaxes on the garage area's best substitute for a comfortable chair. In 1967, racing tires used by NASCAR's Grand National division had some tread. Today, smooth racing "slicks" are used by Winston Cup cars.

the way he did, worked my way through traffic the way he did . . . what I mean is I *tried* to copy him; I still haven't been able to do what he did. But I'm going to keep on trying."

In the 1967 Southern 500 program, Jim Hunter described the "passing of the torch" from father to son:

"In the soft, lingering coolness of sunset, Buck Baker spoke slowly. The old pro, who refuses to let the sun go down on his career, leaned against a pickup truck, flipped a hand in the air and said, 'It was a good feeling . . . running down the backstretch . . . looking in the rearview mirror . . . seeing Buddy come . . . catching the look on his face as he shot past . . . knowing exactly what he meant when he waved.'

"You knew, that afternoon, that a colorful old pro was beginning to see the end of the competitive road for himself. 'You can't do anything nowadays without the backing . . . without the competitive stuff,' said Buck. 'But I'm not worried about me . . . I've been there. I just wanna see Buddy get there . . . and I know he will.'"

This was a year for reflection: 1967. Memories were etched into the minds of those who had experienced events at "The Lady In Black."

Reminiscing about Darlington Raceway, Johnny Hendrix, motorsports editor of the *Charleston News and Courier*, called up images of "that old pile of asphalt, steel and dust, the burnt rubber smell and gas fumes, the people of the place."

The pulse of Darlington Raceway remained steady.

"There are skeptics who say the place doesn't live and breathe like a human being, and hasn't a soul, and isn't vindictive, and good and kind, and all the other things real humans are," Hendrix said. "But we know better. We've walked through that infield on Sunday night before Labor Day and experienced something entirely unique in a world that has taught us to be cynical and skeptical."

"The old ones [drivers] are fading out and new ones are coming in," Hendrix said, "but the old place just sits there in the middle of what used to be somebody's cotton field or something, and twice a year it comes alive and rears up on its hind legs and dares men and pieces of machinery to get out of line."

And 1967 was a year for looking ahead. Paul Goldsmith, Jim Paschal, Dick Hutcherson, and others prepared to face Darlington Raceway.

Paul Goldsmith (Goldy) was described by W. W. Cary as "a successful businessman, a polished airplane pilot, a shrewd race driver, a family man, and a full-time nice guy."

He was a respected test driver. He could take a car to its limits and "come back and tell engineers in their own language what they could do to improve performance."

Jim Paschal was described by Joe Whitlock of the *State* in Columbia, South Carolina, as "a race driver's race driver, with a knack for doing it all—oval course, dirt track, big track, little track and road course—and doing it all with the polish of a well-trained professional. Yet Darlington's unusual and historic layout has never yielded to his talent."

Paschal had been racing at Darlington Raceway since it opened in 1950.

"But Jim Paschal is as stubborn as this old race course," Whitlock said. "If he wins the race he'll smile and go through the ritual that accompanies winning. If he loses, he'll shrug his big shoulders, stoke up a cigar and wait until next time."

Unlike Buddy Baker, Dick Hutcherson did not have a family member as a racing mentor. Hutcherson appeared to be destined for a career in his father's construction business after his time in the Air Force.

"But some buddies of mine bought an old Modified car, and nobody wanted to drive it," Hutcherson said. "I guess I was sorta drafted."

Joe Whitaker, motorsports editor of the *State* in Columbia, South Carolina, said, "Tire dust has been in the smiling Midwesterner's cuff ever since."

"Nothing is easy in a business as fickle as stock car racing," Hutcherson said. "I learned early to live with disappointment, confident that one big win will wash away past failures. I'm not impatient, but I am optimistic. I've been patient, trying to master each superspeedway, and I think I've learned them all now."

In 1967, "ordinary people" had the opportunity to learn the superspeedway at Charlotte. The program for the 1967 Southern 500 included a full-page ad for the National School of Safe High Performance Driving, operated by Curtis Turner at Charlotte Motor Speedway.

Students would learn how to "take care of yourself and your car under such amazing situations as brake failure, blowouts, skidding, jammed accelerator, hydroplaning, spin-outs and other emergencies. You'll learn how to corner properly, flatten out in the stretch, make quick stops, avoid obstacles, and keep safe and complete control of your car under all conditions, day or night."

Turner's instructors included: Sam McQuagg, James Hylton, Dick Hutcherson, Tiny Lund, Elmo Langley, Buddy Baker, Tom Pistone, Wendell Scott, Thomas Mills (Curly), Cale Yarborough, Donnie Allison, Bobby Issac, Glen Wood, Bobby Allison, and Buck Baker.

The high-performance driving course was available to "anyone with a valid driver's license and at least two years of driving experience."

And, finally, 1967 was the last year Tom Kirkland served as Darlington Raceway's track photographer. His photographs captured the heart and soul of this "first generation" of stock car racing. Kirkland's images documented the birth and maturation of that fickle track in South Carolina.

Like the drivers who faced Darlington Raceway's tough corners, Kirkland overcame challenges faced by racing photographers: bulky cameras in the early 1950s; split-second action on the track; long hours in extreme heat and humidity; and constantly changing lighting conditions.

However, as Kirkland has said, he had a love for photography and a love for stock car racing. He had fun shooting the Southern 500 and its related events. He met some interesting people, saw some great racing, preserved many memorable moments on film, and watched a sport grow into a phenomenon.

David Pearson takes a few moments to smoke a cigarette before the 1967 Rebel 400. The cars are lined up on the track in starting position. Pearson's watch shows 1:56. The race started at 2:30 P.M. He shares his tire, but he's alone with his thoughts.

This sequence shows the start of the race, just after the green flag dropped.

Richard Petty won both the Rebel 400 and Southern 500 in 1967. After the Rebel 400 win, Petty is hugged by both Miss Firebird, Winkie Louise, and Miss Southern 500, Beth Bryan, in victory lane.

Epilogue

An ambitious man with a dream and a bulldozer started the whole thing. The origin of modern stock car racing may be traced back to Harold Brasington and his track, Darlington Raceway.

This book has focused on the early days of Darlington Raceway. Although not all of the sport's heroes could be profiled here, the author has attempted to provide a feel for those days when NASCAR racing was young.

The sport of stock car racing grew up that September day in 1950. Several of stock car racing's traditions were born at Darlington Raceway: infield camping for race fans; sharply dressed crew members; two cans of fuel per pit stop; pre-race rituals, including bands, beauty pageants and parties; the format used by NASCAR's truck series (an adaptation of the Monza-type Rebel 300 in 1963); and pilgrimages to racing museums and halls of fame, such as the Joe Weatherly Stock Car Museum and Daytona U.S.A.

The high-speed ballet of today's 18-second pit stops developed because of long races at long tracks. Darlington Raceway hosted the first long race. It was the first long track. Nearly a decade later, the second superspeedway was built at Daytona.

Blue laws that prohibited events such as stock car racing on Sunday were relaxed in 1984, and the Southern 500 was moved from Labor Day to the preceding Sunday.

Darlington Raceway was purchased by International Speedway Corporation in 1982. Improvements have continued to be made at the track.

New grandstands were added in 1997. Because the original grandstands were built close to Highway 34, the new grandstands were built on the back stretch. That meant most race fans would not be able to see the start-finish line. So, the start-finish line was moved across the track. Turn One became Turn Three and Turn Two became Turn Four.

The first race run with the start-finish line on the "wrong" side of the track was the 1997 Southern 500.

Excitement fills the hearts of stock car drivers, crew members, motorsports journalists, and racing fans when they hear the words Darlington Raceway. The challenge of conquering the "Lady in Black" is the same as ever.

Jim Hunter has become president of Darlington Raceway. And that old track in South Carolina continues to test stock car racers' mettle.

With the pedal to the metal, they accept the challenge. If they fail, well, that's racin'. They know Darlington Raceway will be waiting for them—next time.

> *There is no other track on the NASCAR Grand National [now Winston Cup] circuit that asks as much of a driver, mechanic and machine. An error, just one, can put a driver and race car out of the running faster than a scorer can make his mark. There's something about the race track here. Something that drains a driver, mechanic and machine of their competitive juices. But ask Joe Weatherly and Bud Moore [winner and car owner of the seventh Rebel 400, 1963], and they'll tell you, "it gives them back when you win."*
>
> —Jim Hunter
> 1963 Southern 500 souvenir program

Appendix
Race Results

Sources: NASCAR records, Darlington Raceway, Souvenir programs of races at Darlington International Raceway, and Greg Fielden's Forty Years of Stock Car Racing series

AAA Speedway Car Race 1950 [no date available]
Darlington Raceway, South Carolina

Top 10 Finish	Driver
1	Johnny Parsons
2	Bill Schindler
3	Henry Banks
4	Cecil Green
5	Duke Dinsmore
6	Chuck Stevenson
7	Joie Chitwood
8	Walt Faulkner
9	Jack McGrath
10	Lee Wallard

Southern 500 • September 4, 1950
Darlington Raceway, South Carolina

Finish	Start	No.	Driver	Car	Winnings
1	43	98	Johnny Mantz	1950 Plymouth	$10,510
2	67	82	Fireball Roberts	1950 Oldsmobile	$3,500
3	7	22	Red Byron	1950 Cadillac	$2,000
4	23	59	Bill Rexford	1950 Oldsmobile	$1,500
5	15	77	Chuck Mahoney	1950 Mercury	$1,000
6	35	42	Lee Petty	1949 Plymouth	$800
7	38	71	Cotton Owens	1950 Plymouth	$930
8	64	2	Bill Blair	1949 Cadillac	$600
9	44	52	Hershell McGriff	1950 Oldsmobile	$500
10	26	61	George Hartley	1950 Oldsmobile	$450
11	16	9	Tim Flock	1950 Oldsmobile	$400
12	57	44	Johnny Grubb	1950 Plymouth	$350
13	62	26	Dick Linder	1950 Oldsmobile	$300
14	68	89	John DuBoise	1950 Ford	$250
15	72	72	Weldon Adams	1949 Plymouth	$225
16	32	99	Barney Smith	1950 Oldsmobile	$275
17	3	51	Gober Sosebee	1950 Oldsmobile	$290
18	52	39	Elmer Wilson	1949 Plymouth	$100
19	21	4	Joe Eubanks	1950 Mercury	-0-
20	19	43	Shorty York	1950 Buick	-0-
21	51	64	Walt Crawford	1950 Buick	-0-
22	33	-	Murrace Walker	1950 Oldsmobile	-0-
23	48	-	Gene Comstock	1950 Oldsmobile	-0-
24	27	17	Jack White	1950 Ford	-0-
25	71	-	Byron Beatty	1950 Ford	-0-
26	53	-	Bill Widenhouse	1949 Plymouth	-0-
27	4	7	Bob Flock	1950 Oldsmobile	-0-
28	10	47	Fonty Flock	1950 Oldsmobile	-0-
29	13	19	Jack Smith	1950 Oldsmobile	-0-
30	30	34	Pee Wee Martin	1950 Oldsmobile	$100
31	5	-	Lee Morgan	1949 Oldsmobile	-0-
32	8	-	Hub McBride	1950 Mercury	-0-
33	11	-	Slick Smith	1950 Oldsmobile	-0-
34	12	45	Ted Chamberlain	1950 Plymouth	-0-
35	6	-	Virgil Livengood	1950 Oldsmobile	-0-
36	9	-	Billy Carden	1950 Ford	-0-
37	14	37	Bill Snowden	1950 Nash	-0-
38	22	21	Harold Kite	1949 Lincoln	-0-
39	25	49	Glenn Dunnaway	1950 Lincoln	-0-
40	2	25	Jimmy Thompson	1950 Lincoln	$125
41	65	27	Jimmy Florian	1950 Oldsmobile	-0-
42	20	-	Bob Smith	1950 Oldsmobile	-0-
43	24	0	Jimmie Lewallen	1950 Oldsmobile	-0-
44	75	-	Jesse James Taylor	1950 Mercury	-0-
45	29	-	Bub King	1950 Mercury	-0-
46	36	24	Gene Darragh	1950 Hudson	-0-
47	39	-	Roy Bentley	1950 Studebaker	-0-
48	42	-	J.E. Hardie	1950 Studebaker	-0-
49	34	-	Jerry Kemp	1950 Lincoln	-0-
50	46	36	Bill Osborne	1950 Mercury	$100
51	37	-	Carson Dyer	1950 Lincoln	-0-
52	60	33	Wally Campbell	1950 Oldsmobile	$100
53	40	79	Jim Paschal	1950 Ford	-0-
54	45	18	Charles Tidwell	1949 Oldsmobile	$100
55	41	-	Ruel Smith	1950 Pontiac	-0-
56	47	-	Al Keller	1950 Oldsmobile	-0-
57	50	-	Dick Soper	1950 Kaiser	-0-
58	54	-	Pete Keller	1950 Studebaker	-0-
59	56	-	P.E. Godfrey	1949 Lincoln	-0-
60	1	41	Curtis Turner	1950 Oldsmobile	$320
61	49	-	Bob Apperson	1949 Oldsmobile	-0-
62	55	-	Tommy Thompson	1950 Hudson	-0-
63	61	6	Marshall Teague	1950 Lincoln	-0-
64	70	14	Tex Keene	1950 Plymouth	-0-
65	31	-	Clyde Minter	1950 Lincoln	$100
66	74	-	Rollin Smith	1950 Hudson	-0-
67	17	86	Bill Henson	1949 Oldsmobile	$100
68	59	48	Gayle Warren	1949 Oldsmobile	$100
69	28	87	Buck Baker	1949 Oldsmobile	-0-
70	58	46	Ken Wagner	1949 Lincoln	$100
71	18	62	Lloyd Moore	1950 Lincoln	$100
72	73	48	Alton Haddock	1950 Ford	-0-
73	69	-	Jack Yardley	1950 Ford	-0-
74	66	-	Jack Carr	1950 Mercury	-0-
75	63	-	Roscoe Thompson	1949 Oldsmobile	-0-

AAA Speedway Car Race 1951 [no date available]
Darlington Raceway, SC

Top 10 Finish	Driver
1	Walt Faulkner
2	Tony Bettenhausen
3	Cecil Green
4	Bill Mackey
5	Jack McGrath
6	Manuel Ayulo
7	Henry Banks
8	Mike Nazaruk
9	Chuck Stevenson
10	Walt Brown

Southern 500 • September 3, 1951
Darlington Raceway, South Carolina

Finish	Start	No.	Driver	Car	Winnings
1	2	92	Herb Thomas	1951 Hudson	$8,800
2	3	31	Jesse James Taylor	1951 Hudson	$2,800
3	19	17	Buddy Shuman	1951 Ford 8	$1,500
4	5	77	Hershell McGriff	1951 Olds 88	$1,210
5	7	11	Fireball Roberts	1951 Ford	$910
6	38	1	Harold Kite	1951 Olds 88	$800
7	27	46	Leon Sales	1951 Olds 88	$700
8	4	14	Fonty Flock	1951 Olds 88	$600
9	6	16	Bill Snowden	1951 Ford 8	$500
10	55	24	Pap White	1951 Plymouth	$400
11	45	91	Tim Flock	1951 Olds 88	$350
12	16	12	Slick Smith	1950 Olds 88	$240
13	52	34	Jack Goodwin	1951 Plymouth	$300
14	15	8	Billy Carden	1950 Cadillac	$300
15	24	42	Lee Petty	1951 Plymouth	$250
16	51	-	Gober Sosebee	1951 Olds 88	$250
17	47	70	Bud Farrell	1950 Plymouth	$200
18	23	99	Billy Myers	1951 Plymouth	$200
19	80	64	Bill Widenhouse	1951 Plymouth	$150
20	39	18	George Seeger	1951 Studebaker	$150
21	11	4	Gayle Warren	1951 Studebaker	$100
22	30	95	Freddie Farmer	1951 Nash	$100
23	82	71	Cotton Owens	1951 Plymouth	$100
24	60	56	Ed Benedict	1951 Hudson	$100
25	54	83	Red Byron	1951 Ford	$100
26	29	66	Bud Riley	1951 Hudson	$50
27	10	7	Bob Flock	1951 Olds 88	$50
28	62	0	Jimmie Lewallen	1951 Plymouth	$50
29	63	61	Tommy Melvin	1951 Olds 88	$50
30	31	86	Earl Moss	1951 Studebaker	$50
31	25	50	Ewell Weddle	1950 Ford 8	$50
32	48	90	Shorty York	1951 Nash	$50
33	47	6	Marshall Teague	1951 Hudson	$500
34	41	78	Johnny Yountz	1951 Plymouth	$50
35	49	10	Ted Swaim	1950 Ford 8	$50
36	50	67	Jim Fieblekorn	1951 Lincoln	$50
37	21	37	Gene Comstock	1950 Olds 88	$50
38	65	74	Oliver Dial	1951 Chevrolet	$50
39	22	60	Jim Paschal	1950 Ford 8	$50
40	79	32	Reino Tulonen	1951 Henry J	$50
41	61	94	Ted Chamberlain	1951 Plymouth	$50
42	73	96	J.E. Hardie	1951 Ford	$50
43	43	93	Donald Thomas	1951 Plymouth	$50
44	75	9	Iggy Katona	1951 Chrysler	$50
45	70	20	Joe Merola	1951 Olds 88	$50
46	76	33	Dave Anderson	1951 Kaiser	$50
47	57	49	Bob Pronger	1950 Olds 88	$50
48	17	57	Jack Smith	1951 Olds 88	$50
49	78	43	Billy Tibbett	1951 Dodge	$50
50	69	75	Jimmy Warden	1951 Hudson	$50
51	58	5	Gene Darragh	1950 Olds 88	$50
52	53	27	Gwyn Staley	1951 Ford 6	$50
53	72	21	Jim Delaney	1951 Ford	$50

151

Finish	Start	No.	Driver	Car	Winnings
54	33	15	Erick Erickson	1951 Pontiac	$50
55	68	2	Bill Blair	1951 Ford 6	$50
56	18	87	Buck Baker	1951 Ford 6	$50
57	26	41	Curtis Turner	1951 Olds 88	$480
58	40	72	Wade Fields	1951 Plymouth	$50
59	15	22	Lloyd Dane	1951 Ford	$50
60	64	48	Johnny Barker	1951 Studebaker	$50
61	77	44	Buck Baity	1950 Buick	-0-
62	8	28	Ray Chase	1950 Olds 88	-0-
63	18	25	Jimmy Thompson	1951 Ford 8	-0-
64	67	3	Jimmy Ayers	1950 Plymouth	-0-
65	9	38	Frank Gise	1951 Studebaker	-0-
66	32	97	Sandy Lynch	1951 Ford 6	-0-
67	28	80	Bob Johnson	1951 Studebaker	-0-
68	66	89	Herb Trimble	1951 Olds 88	-0-
69	37	55	Bub King	1950 Plymouth	-0-
70	74	40	Tommy Thompson	1951 Nash	-0-
71	34	52	Bill Rexford	1950 Olds 88	-0-
72	81	58	Fred Moore	1951 Mercury	-0-
73	46	26	Weldon Adams	1951 Plymouth	-0-
74	36	47	Murrace Walker	1951 Studebaker	-0-
75	72	82	Joe Eubanks	1951 Olds 88	-0-
76	35	98	Johnny Mantz	1951 Nash	-0-
77	56	39	Rudy Hires	1951 Ford 6	-0-
78	59	35	Sonny Black	1951 Plymouth	-0-
79	13	59	Lloyd Moore	1951 Ford 8	-0-
80	42	19	Lee Connell	1951 Pontiac	-0-
81	20	73	Bobby Booth	1950 Olds 88	-0-
82	1	23	Frank Mundy	1951 Studebaker	-0-

NASCAR Speedway Car Race • May 10, 1952
Darlington Raceway, South Carolina

Finish	Car No.	Driver	Car
1	87	Buck Baker	Cadillac
2	7	Bill Miller	Olds 88
3	38	Tom Cherry	Mercury
4	88	Al Keller	Cadillac
5	74	Bob Jeffries	Hudson
6	2	Jack Smith (102 laps)	
		Tex Keene (46 laps)	Chrysler
7	77	Buddy Shuman	GMC
8	22	Mickey Fenn	Ford
9	48	Sam Waldrop	Hudson
10	27	Jimmy Thompson	Mercury
11	2X	Sam (Red) Ryder	Studebaker
12	24	Jim Sweeney	Olds 88
13	52	Fred Peters	Ford
14	45	Larry Pharer	Nash
15	25	Al (Speedy) Thompson	Ford
16	1	Wally Campbell	Ford
17	33	Steve McGrath	DeSoto
18	10	Tony Bonadies	Chrysler
19	66	Herb Swann	Olds 88
20	77	Lyle Scott	DeSoto
21	5	Dick Rathmann	Ford
22	23	Bill Widenhouse	Hudson

NASCAR Grand National Race • May 10, 1952
Darlington Raceway, South Carolina

Finish	Start	No.	Driver	Car	Winnings
1	4	120	Dick Rathmann	1951 Hudson	$1,000
2	3	91	Tim Flock	1951 Hudson	$700
3	2	14	Fonty Flock	1951 Olds 88	$450
4	9	2	Jimmie Lewallen	1952 Olds 88	$350
5	6	82	Joe Eubanks	1952 Hudson	$200
6	24	72	Donald Thomas	1951 Ford	$150
7	13	42	Lee Petty	1951 Plymouth	$125
8	1	11	Fireball Roberts	1951 Ford	$100
9	8	41	Jim Paschal	1952 Hudson	$75
10	12	7	Frank Mundy	1950 Olds 88	$50
11	11	51	Gober Sosebee	1951 Chrysler	$25
12	10	77	Weldon Adams	1951 Chrysler	$25
13	14	92	Herb Thomas	1952 Hudson	$25
14	19	96	J.E. Hardie	1952 Studebaker	$25
15	3	89	Buck Baker	1952 Hudson	$25
16	15	128	Charles Gattalia	1951 Studebaker	$25
17	17	8	Jack Smith	1951 Studebaker	$25
18	7	22	Perk Brown	1951 Hudson	$25
19	18	21	Speedy Thompson	1951 Ford 6	$25
20	23	17	Bill Widenhouse	1951 Ford 6	$25
21	16	9	Ed Samples	1951 Olds 88	$25
22	2	81	Roscoe Thompson	1951 Olds 88	$25
23	21	99	Leonard Tippett	1951 Hudson	$25
24	20	94	Joe Statton	1951 Nash	$25

NASCAR Modified & Sportsman Race • July 4, 1952
Darlington Raceway, South Carolina

Finish	Driver	Car	Type
1	Curtis Turner	Ford	Spts.
2	Buddy Shuman	Ford	Mod.
3	Fireball Roberts	Ford	Mod.
4	Jimmy Lewallen	Ford	Spts.
5	Joe Eubanks	Ford	Mod.
6	Bob Myers	Ford	Spts.
7	Banjo Matthews	Ford	Mod.
8	Walter Crawford	Hudson	Mod.
9	Billy Carden	Ford	Mod.
10	Bill Myers	Ford	Spts.
11	Elmer Cooper	Ford	Spts.
12	Leon Sales	Ford	Spts.
13	Rudy Hires	Chevrolet	Mod.
14	Bob Quillich	Ford	Mod.
15	Rex Stansell	Plymouth	Mod.
16	Ken Marriott	Lincoln	Mod.
17	Baldy Wilson	Ford	Spts.
18	Herb McBride	Ford	Mod.
19	Jim Paschal	Ford	Spts.
20	Jim Cooper	Ford	Spts.
21	Jimmy Thompson	Ford	Mod.
22	David Ezell	Ford	Spts.
23	Robert Hudson	Ford	Mod.
24	Homer Owens	Ford	Mod.
25	Les Chandler	Ford	Mod.
26	Speedy Thompson	Ford	Mod.
27	Max Tolbert	Ford	Mod.
28	Barney Ross	Ford	Spts.
29	Gene Darrah	Oldsmobile	Mod.
30	Joe Buff	Ford	Mod.
31	Johnny Miller	Ford	Mod.
32	Jack Smith	Ford	Mod.
33	Ralph Earnhardt	Ford	Mod.
34	Frankie Schneider	Ford	Mod.
35	Stan Parnell	Ford	Mod.
36	Slim Rominger	Ford	Spts.
37	Felix McConnell	Ford	Spts.
38	Doug Yates	Ford	Mod.
39	Ed Hansen	Ford	Mod.
40	Richard Riley	Ford	Mod.
41	Bobby Johns	Ford	Spts.
42	Bob Wiesemeyer	Studebaker	Spts.

Southern 500 • September 1, 1952
Darlington Raceway, South Carolina

Finish	Start	No.	Driver	Car	Winnings
1	1	14	Fonty Flock	1952 Olds 88	$9,430
2	42	58	Johnny Patterson	1952 Hudson	$3,000
3	14	92	Herb Thomas	1952 Hudson	$1,590
4	33	55	Bub King	1952 Hudson	$1,230
5	53	16	Banjo Matthews	1952 Hudson	$950
6	8	42	Lee Petty	1951 Plymouth	$800
7	2	82	Joe Eubanks	1952 Hudson	$700
8	3	1	Hershell Buchanan	1952 Nash	$600
9	5	87	Buck Baker	1952 Lincoln	$500
10	50	24	Ray Duhigg	1951 Plymouth	$450
11	16	9	Jack Smith*	1951 Hudson	$420
12	35	69	Rollin Smith	1952 Hudson	$350
13	37	89	Jimmy Thompson	1952 Hudson	$300
14	47	51	Speedy Thompson	1951 Ford	$280
15	48	59	Lloyd Moore	1952 Ford	$250
16	38	53	Joe Weatherly	1952 Hudson	$150
17	43	98	Buddy Shuman	1951 Plymouth	$100
18	41	62	Keith Hamner	1952 Hudson	$90
19	31	25	Clyde Pittinger	1952 Olds 88	$90
20	10	99	Pat Kirkwood	1951 Chrysler	$90
21	56	8	Gene Comstock	1952 Hudson	$90
22	57	25	W.E. Baker, Jr.	1952 Olds 88	$90
23	59	28	Herb Fry	1951 Hudson	$95
24	61	34	Iggy Katona	1951 Plymouth	$75
25	21	77	Dick Passwater	1952 Olds 88	$105
26	23	83	Bill Miller	1951 Ford	$75
27	11	85	Tony Bonadies	1951 Nash Rambler	$325
28	27	66	Donald Thomas	1951 Plymouth	$60
29	55	7	Bob Flock	1951 Hudson	$60
30	12	67	Irvin Blatt	1951 Mercury	$60
31	25	93	Ted Chamberlain	1950 Plymouth	$60
32	9	47	Al Fleming	1952 Willys	$210
33	36	91	Tim Flock**	1952 Hudson	$50
34	?	94	E.C. Ramsey	1951 Ford	$50
35	29	20	Dick Rathmann	1952 Hudson	$460
36	32	75	Al Conroy	1952 Willys	$150
37	66	71	Coleman Lawrence	1950 Plymouth	$50
38	65	79	Charles Weidler	1951 Hudson	$50
39	45	31	Rudy Hires	1952 Hudson	$50
40	40	60	Ralph Liguori	1951 Hudson	$50
41	24	3	Lamar Crabtree	1951 Plymouth	-0-
42	28	30	Johnny Bridgers	1952 Ford	-0-
43	44	57	Tommy Moon	1951 Hudson	-0-
44	17	2	Bill Blair	1952 Olds 88	-0-
45	51	17	June Cleveland	1951 Plymouth	-0-
46	34	52	Joe Guide, Jr.	1951 Hudson	-0-
47	58	61	Lewis Jones	1951 Ford	-0-
48	6	22	Roy Hall	1952 DeSoto	-0-
49	7	11	Fireball Roberts	1951 Ford	-0-
50	20	32	Jimmie Lewallen	1952 Hudson	$20
51	30	74	Pete Kelley	1952 Hudson	-0-
52	46	6	Bobby Myers	1951 Ford	-0-
53	18	18	Bucky Sager	1952 Hudson	-0-
54	15	46	Bob Pronger	1952 Olds 88	-0-
55	39	43	Larry Mann	1952 Hudson	-0-
56	63	54	Weldon Adams	1951 Plymouth	-0-
57	52	26	Jimmy Ingram	1951 Nash	-0-
58	60	27	Gwyn Staley	1952 Ford	-0-
59	26	21	Johnny Gouveia	1951 Plymouth	-0-
60	13	40	Tommy Thompson	1952 Hudson	$200
61	49	41	Curtis Turner	1952 Olds 88	-0-
62	54	5	Gene Darragh	1952 Hudson	-0-
63	?	15	Merritt Brown	1951 Studebaker	-0-
64	19	4	Slick Smith	1951 Olds 88	$50
65	4	19	Clyde Minter	1952 Packard	-0-
66	22	12	Jim Paschal	1952 Olds 88	-0-

*was relieved by Tim Flock   **relieved Jack Smith

Modified and Sportsman • July 4, 1953
NASCAR 200-Mile Race
Darlington Raceway, South Carolina

Finish	Driver	Car	Type
1	Junior Johnson	1937 Ford	Mod.
2	Cotton Owens	1937 Plymouth	Mod.
3	Joe Weatherly	1939 Ford	Mod.
4	Banjo Matthews	1935 Ford	Mod.
5	Milt Hartlauf	1937 Ford	Mod.
6	Buddy Shuman	1939 Ford	Mod.
7	Buck Baker	1935 Oldsmobile	Spts.
8	Joe Eubanks	1937 Ford	Mod.
9	Bobby Myers	1939 Ford	Spts.
10	Earl Moss	1937 Ford	Mod.
11	Tommy Thompson	1939 Ford	Mod.
12	Roscoe Thompson	1939 Ford	Mod.
13	Ted Swaim	1939 Ford	Spts.
14	Sonny Palmer	1937 Ford	Mod.
15	Banks Simpson	1939 Ford	Mod.
16	Slick Smith	1939 Ford	Mod.
17	Speedy Thompson	1934 Ford	Mod.
18	Rudy Hires	1939 Ford	Mod.
19	Pee Wee Jones	1937 Ford	Spts.
20	Jimmy Lewallen	1939 Ford	Mod.
21	Tommy Moon	1939 Ford	Mod.
22	Glenn Burthie	1937 Ford	Mod.
23	E.H. Weddle	1937 Ford	Spts.
24	Tommy Byrnes	1939 Ford	Mod.
25	Pat Kenny	1939 Ford	Mod.
26	Bobby Johns	1935 Ford	Mod.
27	Paul Sanborn	1937 Ford	Mod.
28	Harold Smith	1939 Ford	Spts.
29	Allan Clarke	1937 Ford	Mod.
30	Glenn Wood	1937 Ford	Spts.
31	Bill Widenhouse	1939 Ford	Mod.
32	Ned Jarrett	1937 Ford	Spts.
33	Max Talbort	1937 Ford	Mod.
34	Fireball Roberts	1935 Ford	Mod.
35	Runt Harris	1939 Ford	Mod.
36	Jimmy Rowland	1939 Ford	Mod.
37	Bill Warren	1938 Ford	Spts.
38	Gwyn Staley	1937 Ford	Spts.
39	C.P. McDonald	1939 Ford	Spts.
40	LeRoy Hicks	1939 Ford	Mod.
41	Bobby McGinnis	1938 Ford	Spts.
42	Fletcher Hornsby	1939 Ford	Mod.
43	C.I. Grant	1939 Chevrolet	Mod.
44	Carl Burris	1939 Ford	Mod.
45	Claude Timms	1935 Ford	Mod.
46	Ralph Ligouri	1938 Ford	Mod.
47	Cecil Riner	1939 Ford	Mod.
48	Hassell Reid	1938 Ford	Mod.
49	Red Hudson	1939 Ford	Mod.
50	Jack Walters	1948 Ford	Mod.
51	Sandy Sanders	1935 Ford	Mod.
52	Oliver Michael	1939 Ford	Mod.
53	Billy Evans	1939 Ford	Mod.
54	Weldon Adams	1935 Ford	Mod.
55	Fonty Flock	1939 Ford	Mod.
56	Bob Wheatley	1937 Ford	Mod.
57	Bob Harkey	1939 Ford	Mod.
58	Johnny Dodson	1939 Ford	Mod.
59	Ed Clements	1938 Ford	Mod.
60	Homer Owens	1939 Ford	Mod.
61	Shorty York	1939 Ford	Mod.
62	David Ezell	1939 Ford	Mod.
63	Curtis Turner	1939 Ford	Mod.
64	Jim Cooper	1937 Ford	Mod.

Southern 500 • September 7, 1953
Darlington Raceway, South Carolina

Finish	Start	No.	Driver	Car	Winnings
1	7	87	Buck Baker	1953 Olds 88	$6,285
2	1	14	Fonty Flock	1953 Hudson	$3,040
3	10	44	Curtis Turner	1953 Olds 88	$1,500
4	13	49	Dick Meyer	1953 Dodge	$1,000
5	4	92	Herb Thomas	1953 Hudson	$1,550
6	16	80	Jim Paschal	1953 Dodge	$800
7	19	46	Speedy Thompson	1953 Olds 88	$750
8	5	56	Donald Thomas*	1953 Hudson	$700
9	22	00	Dick Passwater	1953 Olds 88	$630
10	9	91	Tim Flock	1953 Hudson	$520
11	44	42	Lee Petty	1953 Dodge	$450
12	24	67	Elton Hildreth	1953 Nash	$400
13	21	6	Jimmie Lewallen	1953 Olds 88	$350
14	8	89	Buddy Shuman	1953 Hudson	$345
15	32	21	Neil Roberts	1953 Chrysler	$300
16	25	22	George Osborne	1953 Hudson	$275
17	29	7	Lloyd Hulette	1953 Buick	$250
18	30	8	Gene Comstock	1953 Hudson	$225
19	33	71	Fred Dove	1951 Ford 6	$200
20	50	18	Bobby Myers	1953 Olds 88	$190
21	55	55	Bub King	1953 Packard	$175
22	34	60	Tyre Rakestraw**	1953 Chevrolet	$160
23	47	51	Gober Sosebee	1952 Olds	$150
24	39	50	Bob Weatherly	1952 Plymouth	$140
25	37	97	Lacy Jackson	1952 Hudson	$130
26	48	30	Johnny Bridges	1951 Ford	$120
27	40	10	Chet Williams	1951 Ford	$110
28	15	06	Marvin Panch	1953 Dodge	$110
29	50	?	Elmer Cooper	1953 Nash Ramb.	$110
30	22	08	Arden Mounts	1953 Hudson	$110
31	12	9	Jim Reed	1953 Hudson	$110
32	38	99	Matt Gowen	1953 Plymouth	$110
33	45	2	Bill Blair	1953 Olds 88	$110
34	20	23	Mike Magill	1953 Lincoln	$110
35	54	25	Bill Norton	1952 Olds 88	$110
36	14	47	Otis Martin	1953 Plymouth	$110
37	28	73	Bill Widenhouse	1953 Nash Amb.	$110
38	26	75	Junior Johnson	1953 Olds Holiday	$110
39	44	16	Weldon Adams	1951 Ford	$110
40	35	74	J.L. Justice	1952 Ford	$110
41	56	?	Bob Hunter	1953 Olds 88	$105
42	3	120	Dick Rathmann	1953 Hudson	$155
43	42	4	Slick Smith	1953 Olds 88	$105
44	31	77	Dick Allwine	1953 Chevrolet	$105
45	6	11	Fireball Roberts	1953 Olds 88	$340
46	19	13	Emory Lewis	1953 Olds 88	$105
47	53	19	Clyde Minter	1953 Mercury	$105
48	49	45	Ben Dixon***	1952 Hudson	$105
49	57	?	Lonnie Bragg	1952 Hudson	$105
50	36	88	Laird Bruner	1953 Olds 88	$105
51	58	?	Joe Guide, Jr.	1952 Hudson	$100
52	18	58	Johnny Patterson	1953 Hudson	$120
53	51	48	Slim Rominger	1949 Lincoln	$100
54	11	45	Ralph Liguori	1953 Lincoln	$100
55	27	84	Gayle Warren	1953 Studebaker	$100
56	2	82	Joe Eubanks	1952 Hudson	$100
57	43	33	Pop McGinnis	1952 Hudson	$100
58	46	?	Merritt Brown	1953 Studebaker	$100
59	52	79	Ned Jarrett	1950 Olds 88	$100

*was relieved by Dick Rathmann   **was relieved by Slick Smith
***was relieved by Ermon Rush

AAA Speedway Car Race • 1954 [no date available]
Darlington Raceway, South Carolina

Top 10 Finish	Driver
1	Manuel Ayulo
2	Jimmy Reece
3	Jimmy Bryan
4	Johnny Tolan
5	Jerry Hoyt
6	Art Cross
7	Joe Sostilio
8	Sam Hanks
9	Duane Carter
10	Pat O'Connor

Modified and Sportsman NASCAR 200-Mile Race
July 4, 1954 • Darlington Raceway, South Carolina
Top 20

Finish	Driver	Car	Class	Winnings
1	Fireball Roberts	Cadillac	Mod.	$1,880
2	Curtis Turner	Lincoln	Mod.	$700
3	Bill Widenhouse	Cadillac	Mod.	$550
4	Cotton Hodges	Chrysler	Mod.	$450
5	Herb Thomas	Ford	Mod.	$400
6	Earl Moss	Lincoln	Mod.	$350
7	Joe Weatherly	Ford	Mod.	$300
8	Dick Blackwell	Dodge	Spts.	$500
9	Sonny Black	Olds	Mod.	$225
10	Jimmy Roland	Ford	Spts.	$350
11	David Ezell	Ford	Spts.	$250
12	Ralph Moody	Chrysler	Mod.	$125
13	Jimmy Thompson	Mercury	Spts.	$100
14	Billy Myers	Ford	Spts.	$75
15	Rex White	Ford	Mod.	$75
16	Pee Wee Jones	Lincoln	Spts.	$75
17	Dick Joslin	Ford	Spts.	$75
18	Ray Platte	GMC	Mod.	$75
19	Buck Baker	Ford	Mod.	$75
20	George Reichle	Ford	Spts.	$75

Southern 500 • September 6, 1954
Darlington Raceway, South Carolina

Finish	Start	No.	Driver	Car	Winnings
1	23	92	Herb Thomas	1954 Hudson	$6,830
2	17	44	Curtis Turner	1952 Olds 88	$6,245
3	24	98	Marvin Panch	1954 Dodge	$2,155
4	27	58	Johnny Patterson	1954 Mercury	$1,165
5	34	88	Jim Paschal	1954 Olds 88	$975
6	7	40	John Soares	1954 Dodge	$855
7	2	25	Fireball Roberts	1953 Olds 88	$730
8	25	1	Gwyn Staley	1954 Cadillac	$670
9	40	13	Joel Million	1953 Olds 88	$600
10	38	12	Speedy Thompson	1954 Buick	$550
11	21	18	Arden Mounts	1954 Hudson	$500
12	41	53	Elmo Langley	1954 Olds 88	$450
13	9	8	Gene Comstock	1952 Hudson	$400
14	4	28	Eddie Skinner	1953 Olds 88	$350
15	14	82	Joe Eubanks	1951 Hudson	$325
16	50	1	Elton Hildreth	1953 Nash	$300
17	28	17	Bill Widenhouse	1954 Mercury	$275
18	31	47	Harvey Eakin	1953 Nash	$250
19	6	97	Bill Amick	1954 Olds 88	$225
20	11	64	Charlie Crogar	1951 Plymouth	$280
21	19	32	Art Watts	1954 Hudson	$175
22	12	11	George Parrish	1953 Studebaker	$160
23	29	21	Laird Bruner	1954 Olds 88	$150
24	35	27	Jim Gillette	1952 Plymouth	$140

Finish	Start	No.	Driver	Car	Winnings
25	42	48	Otis Martin	1954 Chrysler	$130
26	32	85	Walt Harvey	1950 Ford	$120
27	37	16	Buck Mason	1951 Plymouth	$110
28	30	70	Charles Brinkley	1951 Hudson	$100
29	43	20	Van Vari Wey	1954 Ford	$120
30	15	6	Ralph Liguori	1954 Dodge	$120
31	10	93	Ted Chamberlain	1953 Chrysler	$75
32	48	55	Frank Stutz	1950 Ford	$75
33	5	26	Dave Terrell	1954 Dodge	$75
34	16	83	Cotton Owens	1951 Hudson	$75
35	22	33	Pop McGinnis	1953 Hudson	$115
36	44	71	Dean Pelton	1950 Ford	$75
37	47	15	Joe Sheppard	1954 Ford	$75
38	13	42	Lee Petty	1954 Chrysler	$75
39	39	23	Erick Erickson	1954 Buick	$75
40	8	4	Ken Fisher	1954 Hudson	$75
41	18	5	Jimmie Lewallen	1954 Mercury	$75
42	20	29	Dink Widenhouse	1953 Olds 88	$75
43	26	10	Blackie Pitt	1954 Olds 88	$75
44	1	87	Buck Baker	1954 Olds 88	$465
45	3	14	Hershell McGriff	1954 Olds 88	$95
46	49	20	John McGinley	1953 Hudson	$75
47	46	43	Danny Lettner	1951 Hudson	$75
48	33	90	Bob Welborn	1953 Dodge	$75
49	45	79	Hassel Reid	1949 Plymouth	$75
50	36	75	Jimmy Thompson	1952 Olds 88	$75

Southern 500 • September 5, 1955
Darlington Raceway, South Carolina
[Note: The only race in 1955]

Finish	Start	No.	Driver	Car	Winnings
1	8	92	Herb Thomas	1955 Chevrolet	$7,480
2	21	7	Jim Reed	1955 Chevrolet	$1,550
3	6	16	Tim Flock	1955 Chrysler	$2,500
4	24	2	Gwyn Staley	1955 Chevrolet	$1,300
5	30	96	Larry Flynn	1955 Ford	$1,175
6	2	89	Buck Baker	1955 Buick	$1,055
7	26	93	Lou Spear	1955 Chevrolet	$700
8	27	70	Cotton Owens	1955 Chevrolet	$600
9	4	25	Bill Widenhouse	1955 Chevrolet	$445
10	41	4	Jimmy Massey	1955 Chevrolet	$400
11	20	20	Banks Simpson	1955 Buick	$475
12	5	82	Joe Eubanks	1955 Oldsmobile	$550
13	45	44	Marvin Panch	1955 Chevrolet	$300
14	33	54	Nace Mattingly	1955 Ford	$350
15	44	88	Jimmie Lewallen	1955 Oldsmobile	$335
16	35	6	Ralph Liguori	1955 Mercury	$400
17	13	84	Banjo Matthews	1955 Oldsmobile	$245
18	37	98	Dave Terrell	1955 Oldsmobile	$165
19	29	17	Russ "Bud" Graham	1955 Chevrolet	$155
20	18	51	Bill Champion	1955 Buick	$195
21	25	42	Lee Petty	1955 Dodge	$335
22	46	68	Johnny Patterson	1955 Mercury	$225
23	34	46	Billy Myers	1955 Chevrolet	$115
24	48	95	Lloyd Moore	1955 Ford	$160
25	32	35	Ray Platte	1955 Chevrolet	$100
26	38	22	Bill Blair	1955 Oldsmobile	$90
27	43	24	Bobby Waddell	1955 Chevrolet	$75
28	31	59	Blackie Pitt	1955 Ford	$75
29	52	12	Jimmy Thompson (NC)	1955 Plymouth	$275
30	69	49	Bob Welborn	1955 Chevrolet	$75
31	61	62	Ewell Hatfield	1955 Chevrolet	$60
32	50	50	Roy Bentley	1955 Chevrolet	$60
33	7	9	Joe Weatherly	1955 Ford	$1,500
34	10	78	Jim Paschal	1955 Oldsmobile	$60
35	59	58	Bill Bowman	1954 Nash	$260
36	17	55	Junior Johnson	1955 Oldsmobile	$60
37	47	30	Ned Jarrett	1955 Pontiac	$260
38	57	61	Ed Bergin	1955 Dodge	$160
39	9	8	Billy Carden	1955 Buick	$60
40	55	78	Tojo Stephens	1955 Chevrolet	$60
41	62	43	Possum Jones	1955 Chevrolet	$60
42	42	28	Eddie Skinner	1955 Oldsmobile	$60
43	51	71	Harold Kite	1955 Oldsmobile	$60
44	36	10	Van Vari Wey	1955 Ford	$60
45	3	87	Speedy Thompson	1954 Oldsmobile	$80
46	22	56	Fred Johnson	1955 Cadillac	$260
47	53	37	Dutch Cox	1955 Pontiac	$150
48	58	81	Gene Comstock	1954 Hudson	$250
49	66	94	Clarence DeZalia	1954 Ford	$50
50	23	77	Dick Allwine	1955 Chevrolet	$50
51	11	36	Fonty Flock	1955 Chrysler	$1,040
52	16	40	Gene Simpson	1955 Buick	$50
53	19	34	Dick Beaty	1955 Ford	$50
54	67	32	Jim Thompson (WV)	1953 Hudson	$150
55	40	23	Don Duckworth	1955 Chevrolet	$50
56	49	18	Arden Mounts	1954 Hudson	$100
57	28	15	Jimmy Roland	1955 Chevrolet	$50
58	15	99	Curtis Turner	1955 Ford	$190
59	54	76	Elmo Langley	1955 Dodge	$100
60	14	91	Donald Thomas	1955 Buick	$50
61	39	14	Slick Smith	1955 Chevrolet	$50
62	12	3	Dick Rathmann	1955 Chrysler	$130
63	60	21	Bud Rackley	1955 Oldsmobile	$50
64	65	41	Tommy Thompson	1955 Ford	$50
65	58	19	Gordon Smith	1955 Chevrolet	$50
66	1	M-1	Fireball Roberts	1955 Buick	$140
67	63	33	Pop McGinnis	1955 Chevrolet	$50
68	56	460	Ed Cole	1955 Plymouth	$150
69	64	11	George Parrish	1953 Studebaker	$250

USAC Big Car Race, "Pee Dee 200" • July 4, 1956
Darlington Raceway, South Carolina

Finish	Driver
1	Pat O'Connor
2	Jack Turner
3	Johnny Boyd
4	G. Amick
5	Pat Flaherty
6	E. Elisian
7	Elmer George
8	Jimmy Bryan
9	Johnny Thompson
10	Don Freeland
11	J. Rathmann
12	Jimmy Reece
13	A. Linden
14	B. Cheesbourg
15	Dick Rathmann
16	K. Gottshalk
17	E. Motter
18	E. Russo
19	R. Ward
20	G. Force
21	E. Sachs
22	G. Hartley
23	B. Garrett

Southern 500 • September 3, 1956
Darlington Raceway, South Carolina

Finish	Start	No.	Driver	Car	Winnings
1	11	99	Curtis Turner	1956 Ford	$11,750
2	1	57	Speedy Thompson	1956 Chrysler	$5,000
3	2	8	Marvin Panch	1956 Ford	$3,370
4	23	7	Jim Reed	1956 Chevrolet	$1,850
5	4	3	Paul Goldsmith	1956 Chevrolet	$1,300
6	17	26	Jim Paschal	1956 Mercury	$1,850
7	3	97	Bill Amick	1956 Ford	$1,020
8	16	9	Joe Weatherly	1956 Ford	$900
9	30	47	Bobby Johns	1956 Chevrolet	$700
10	20	93	Pat Kirkwood	1956 Pontiac	$550
11	28	10	Rex White	1956 Chevrolet	$400
12	15	86	Tim Flock	1956 Ford	$490
13	22	61	Roz Howard	1956 Chevrolet	$250
14	25	38	Johnny Patterson	1956 Chevrolet	$225
15	35	32	Junior Johnson	1956 Chevrolet	$200
16	14	14	Billy Myers	1956 Mercury	$300
17	68	35	Lee Petty	1956 Ford	$175
18	39	80	Harold Hardesty	1956 Oldsmobile	$350
19	42	81	Elmo Langley	1956 Chevrolet	$140
20	46	43	Shorty York	1956 Ford	$130
21	19	31	Bill Champion	1956 Ford	$120
22	65	69	Possum Jones	1956 Chevrolet	$110
23	57	11	Emanuel Zervakis	1956 Chevrolet	$100
24	54	16	Tiny Lund	1956 Chevrolet	$100
25	45	64	Johnny Allen	1956 Plymouth	$300
26	6	87	Buck Baker	1956 Chrysler	$225
27	53	91	Jack Smith	1956 Chevrolet	$75
28	36	19	Billy Carden	1956 Ford	$75
29	24	75	Bill Blair	1956 Mercury	$125
30	33	63	Sherman Utsman	1956 Chevrolet	$75
31	64	65	Lou Spears	1956 Plymouth	$150
32	50	60	Brownie King	1956 Chevrolet	$50
33	9	82	Joe Eubanks	1956 Ford	$50
34	66	48	Allen Adkins	1956 Ford	$50
35	43	89	Tom Lupo	1956 Ford	$50
36	29	21	Gene Bergin	1956 Dodge	$250
37	31	88	Ralph Liguori	1956 Oldsmobile	$150
38	7	27	Frank Mundy	1956 Dodge	$180
39	40	66	Harvey Henderson	1956 Ford	$50
40	61	34	Dick Beaty	1956 Ford	$50
41	67	84	Judge Rider	1956 Ford	$50
42	52	23	Wade Fields	1956 Ford	$50
43	56	54	Bill Brown	1955 Buick	$250
44	53	73	Larry Flynn	1956 Buick	$150
45	62	83	Johnny Dodson	1956 Chevrolet	$50
46	63	59	Blackie Pitt	1956 Plymouth	$100
47	51	6	Pat Grogan	1956 Mercury	$50
48	47	30	Clyde Palmer	1956 Plymouth	$50
49	5	92	Herb Thomas	1956 Chevrolet	$50
50	18	1	Parnelli Jones	1956 Ford	$70
51	13	22	Fireball Roberts	1956 Ford	$160
52	44	44	Ray Hendrick	1956 Chevrolet	$50
53	10	52	Bill Widenhouse	1956 Ford	$50
54	27	29	Dink Widenhouse	1956 Ford	$50
55	48	50	Roy Bentley	1956 Ford	$50
56	58	24	Ken Love	1956 Ford	$50
57	8	12	Ralph Moody	1956 Ford	$70
58	12	15	Fonty Flock	1956 Mercury	$80
59	32	98	Danny Letner	1956 Dodge	$100
60	37	40	Don Oldenberg	1956 Plymouth	$50
61	34	76	Bobby Myers	1956 Mercury	$50
62	21	95	Bob Duell	1956 Ford	$50
63	60	51	Nace Mattingly	1956 Ford	$50
64	41	5	Pee Wee Jones	1956 Dodge	$50
65	26	2	Gwyn Staley	1956 Chevrolet	$50

Finish	Start	No.	Driver	Car	Winnings
66	49	25	Doug Yates	1956 Chevrolet	$50
67	79	72	Peck Peckham	1955 Chevrolet	$50
68	38	17	Bud Graham	1956 Chevrolet	$50
69	69	13	Jesse James Taylor	1956 Ford	$50
70	50	18	Arden Mounts	1956 Pontiac	$50

Rebel 300 • May 12, 1957
Darlington Raceway, South Carolina

Finish	Start	No.	Driver	Car	Winnings
1	4	22	Fireball Roberts	1957 Ford	$2,300
2	7	15	Tim Flock	1957 Mercury	$1,500
3	12	4	Bobby Myers	1956 Mercury	$1,250
4	13	49	Bob Welborn	1957 Chevrolet	$950
5	9	42	Lee Petty	1957 Oldsmobile	$700
6	18	46	Jack Smith	1957 Chevrolet	$650
7	24	10	Roger Baldwin	1956 Ford	$600
8	20	1A	Whitey Norman	1956 Ford	$500
9	10	88	Johnny Dodson	1957 Oldsmobile	$450
10	23	76	Larry Frank	1956 Chevrolet	$350
11	25	44	Al Tasnady	1957 Plymouth	$300
12	15	34	Gwyn Staley	1957 Plymouth	$250
13	19	86	Don Oldenberg	1957 Plymouth	$225
14	22	33	Jim Massey	1957 Plymouth	$225
15	27	20	Jimmy Thompson	1956 Ford	$200
16	26	41	Art Brinkley	1956 Plymouth	$200
17	14	21	Glen Wood	1957 Ford	$200
18	1	3	Paul Goldsmith	1957 Ford	$150
19	5	14	Billy Myers	1957 Mercury	$150
20	2	12	Joe Weatherly	1957 Ford	$100
21	3	26	Curtis Turner	1957 Ford	$100
22	6	98	Marvin Panch	1957 Ford	$100
23	8	97	Bill Amick	1957 Ford	$100
24	21	87	Buck Baker	1957 Chevrolet	$100
25	16	48	Possum Jones	1957 Chevrolet	$100
26	11	39	Dick Beaty	1956 Ford	$100
27	17	75	Ken Rush	1956 Mercury	$100

Southern 500 • September 2, 1957
Darlington Raceway, South Carolina

Finish	Start	No.	Driver	Car	Winnings
1	7	46	Speedy Thompson	1957 Chevrolet	$13,590
2	1	6	Cotton Owens	1957 Pontiac	$6,100
3	32	98	Marvin Panch	1957 Ford	$3,745
4	12	7	Jim Reed	1957 Ford	$2,155
5	9	87	Buck Baker	1957 Chevrolet	$1,650
6	45	2	Billy Carden	1957 Chevrolet	$1,225
7	29	14	Billy Myers	1957 Ford	$1,125
8	25	40	Johnny Mackison	1957 Ford	$975
9	48	48	Possum Jones	1957 Chevrolet	$775
10	28	47	Jack Smith	1957 Chevrolet	$785
11	3	31	Curtis Turner	1957 Ford	$1,060
12	27	64	Johnny Allen	1957 Plymouth	$600
13	17	34	Dick Beaty	1956 Ford	$350
14	4	80	Jimmie Lewallen	1957 Pontiac	$370
15	34	45	Eddie Pagan	1957 Ford	$250
16	23	77	Bobby Johns	1956 Ford	$225
17	26	20	Jimmy Thompson	1956 Ford	$225
18	38	54	Nace Mattingly	1957 Ford	$200
19	37	74	L.D. Austin	1956 Chevrolet	$200
20	11	55	Tiny Lund	1957 Pontiac	$300
21	31	32	Brownie King	1957 Chevrolet	$150
22	35	96	Bobby Keck	1957 Chevrolet	$150
23	41	51	Roy Tyner	1956 Ford	$150
24	8	42	Lee Petty	1957 Oldsmobile	$750
25	42	71	George Parrish	1956 Studebaker	$350
26	33	12	Marvin Porter	1957 Ford	$100
27	30	10	Whitey Norman	1956 Ford	$100
28	20	44	Rex White	1957 Chevrolet	$100
29	19	95	Bob Duell	1957 Ford	$100
30	49	13	Peck Peckham	1956 Chevrolet	$100
31	39	35	Bill Champion	1956 Ford	$100
32	18	97	Bill Amick	1957 Ford	$150
33	10	22	Fireball Roberts	1957 Ford	$460
34	22	11	Parnelli Jones	1957 Ford	$100
35	50	75	Jim Paschal	1957 Ford	$100
36	36	17	Shorty York	1957 Mercury	$300
37	16	89	Joe Caspolich	1957 Ford	$200
38	46	26	Bill Blair	1957 Ford	$100
39	24	90	Runt Harris	1957 Chevrolet	$100
40	14	9	Joe Weatherly	1957 Ford	$130
41	13	84	Banjo Matthews	1957 Ford	$120
42	44	30	Cale Yarborough	1957 Pontiac	$100
43	2	4	Bobby Myers	1957 Oldsmobile	$260
44	6	3	Paul Goldsmith	1957 Ford	$200
45	43	88	Chuck Hansen	1957 Chevrolet	$100
46	21	38	Gwyn Staley	1957 Chevrolet	$100
47	5	62	Frankie Schneider	1957 Chevrolet	$100
48	15	92	Fonty Flock	1957 Pontiac	$100
49	40	68	Neil Castles	1956 Ford	$100
50	47	41	T.A. Toomes	1956 Dodge	$300

Rebel 300 • May 10, 1958
Darlington Raceway, South Carolina

Finish	Start	No.	Driver	Car	Winnings
1	12	26	Curtis Turner	1958 Ford	$5,000
2	10	12	Joe Weatherly	1958 Ford	$2,650
3	2	98	Marvin Panch	1958 Ford	$1,850
4	11	45	Eddie Pagan	1958 Ford	$1,075
5	1	22	Fireball Roberts	1957 Chevrolet	$950
6	5	49	Bob Welborn	1957 Chevrolet	$825
7	4	62	Frank Schneider	1957 Chevrolet	$625
8	16	47	Jack Smith	1958 Pontiac	$525
9	20	76	Larry Frank	1957 Chevrolet	$450
10	13	23	John Mackison	1957 Mercury	$350
11	6	14	Tiny Lund	1957 Mercury	$300
12	30	39	Billy Carden	1957 Chevrolet	$250
13	14	87	Buck Baker	1958 Chevrolet	$225
14	18	99	Shorty Rollins	1958 Ford	$200
15	7	90	Emanuel Zervakis	1957 Chevrolet	$200
16	21	52	Shorty York	1957 Ford	$175
17	15	56	Bill Morton	1957 Ford	$175
18	25	32	Brownie King	1957 Chevrolet	$150
19	28	30	Don Gray	1957 Chevrolet	$150
20	22	86	Neil Castles	1956 Ford	$150
21	31	57	Bill Rafter	1956 Dodge	$100
22	29	78	Shep Langdon	1956 Ford	$100
23	17	95	Dick Beaty	1958 Ford	$100
24	19	2	Bobby Lee	1958 Ford	$100
25	26	34	Johnny Allen	1957 Ford	$100
26	3	2	Cotton Owens	1958 Pontiac	$100
27	23	48	Possum Jones	1957 Chevrolet	$100
28	24	66	Roy Tyner	1958 Plymouth	$100
29	9	42	Lee Petty	1957 Oldsmobile	$150
30	27	25	J.V. Hamby	1956 Chevrolet	$100
31	8	44	Ken Rush	1957 Chevrolet	$100

Southern 500 • September 1, 1958
Darlington Raceway, South Carolina

Finish	Start	No.	Driver	Car	Winnings
1	2	22	Fireball Roberts	1957 Chevrolet	$13,220
2	7	87	Buck Baker	1957 Chevrolet	$5,750
3	8	99	Shorty Rollins	1958 Ford	$3,815
4	17	46	Jimmy Thompson	1957 Chevrolet	$1,995
5	20	98	Marvin Panch	1958 Ford	$1,525
6	25	49	Bob Welborn	1957 Chevrolet	$1,150
7	13	40	Rex White	1958 Chevrolet	$1,045
8	34	30	Doug Cox	1957 Ford	$925
9	23	95	Bob Duell	1957 Ford	$775
10	21	36	Herb Estes	1957 Ford	$675
11	28	11	Junior Johnson	1957 Ford	$500
12	33	66	Roy Tyner	1958 Plymouth	$400
13	29	92	Wilbur Rakestraw	1957 Ford	$300
14	19	1	Speedy Thompson	1958 Chevrolet	$310
15	30	44	Lloyd Dane	1957 Ford	$250
16	12	86	G.C. Spencer	1957 Chevrolet	$315
17	35	48	Possum Jones	1957 Chevrolet	$225
18	22	97	Parnelli Jones	1957 Ford	$200
19	5	42	Lee Petty	1957 Oldsmobile	$345
20	36	25	Gene White	1957 Chevrolet	$200
21	31	15	Jim Paschal	1957 Ford	$150
22	10	19	Herman Beam	1957 Chevrolet	$190
23	15	77	Bobby Johns	1957 Chevrolet	$150
24	18	88	Tiny Lund	1958 Ford	$230
25	41	94	Clarence DeZalia	1956 Ford	$150
26	48	33	Al White	1958 Ford	$100
27	43	85	Carl Tyler	1957 Ford	$100
28	37	2	Bobby Lee	1958 Ford	$100
29	3	12	Joe Weatherly	1958 Ford	$265
30	45	74	L.D. Austin	1957 Ford	$100
31	14	47	Jack Smith	1958 Pontiac	$100
32	16	43	Jim Reed	1957 Oldsmobile	$315
33	4	26	Curtis Turner	1958 Ford	$1,350
34	24	8	Eddie Gray	1957 Ford	$100
35	6	6	Joe Eubanks	1957 Pontiac	$380
36	1	45	Eddie Pagan	1958 Ford	$100
37	47	9	Jesse James Taylor	1956 Ford	$100
38	38	89	Marvin Porter	1957 Ford	$100
39	11	24	Larry Frank	1957 Chevrolet	$275
40	32	14	George Dunn	1957 Mercury	$100
41	27	10	Reds Kagle	1957 Ford	$100
42	26	90	Emanuel Zervakis	1957 Chevrolet	$100
43	46	5	Cotton Owens	1957 Dodge	$100
44	42	31	Bob Bolheimer	1958 Chevrolet	$100
45	44	81	Harvey Hege	1957 Ford	$100
46	39	60	Don Kimberling	1958 Chevrolet	$100
47	9	55	Jimmy Massey	1957 Pontiac	$100
48	40	84	Bob Perry	1957 Ford	$100

Rebel 300 • May 9, 1959
Darlington Raceway, South Carolina [Incomplete data]

Finish	Driver	Car
1	Fireball Roberts	Chevrolet
2	Joe Weatherly	Thunderbird
3	Larry Frank	Chevrolet
4	Bob Burdick	Thunderbird
5	Rex White	Chevrolet
6	Jim Reed	Chevrolet
7	Joe Lee Johnson	Chevrolet
8	Shorty Rollins	Ford
9	Johnny Allen	Chevrolet
10	Joe Eubanks	Ford
11	Roy Tyner	
12	Johnny Beauchamp	
13	Bob Welborn	
14	Ken Rush	
15	Richard Petty	
16	Lee Petty	
17	Bobby Johns	

Finish	Driver	Car
18	G.C. Spencer	
19	Brownie King	
20	George Green	
21	Gene White	
22	Neil Castles	
23	Herman Beam	
24	Fritz Wilson	
25	Tommy Irwin	
26	Buck Baker	
27	Shep Langdon	
28	Curtis Turner	
29	Buck Brigance	
30	Jack Smith	
31	Bobby Lee	
32	Wilbur Rakestraw	
33	Elmo Langley	
34	Tom Pistone	

Southern 500 • September 7, 1959
Darlington Raceway, South Carolina

Finish	Start	No.	Driver	Car	Winnings
1	14	7	Jim Reed	1957 Chevrolet	$17,250
2	5	73	Bob Burdick*	1959 Thunderbird	$7,760
3	22	72	Bobby Johns	1957 Chevrolet	$4,760
4	6	43	Richard Petty**	1959 Plymouth	$2,830
5	16	36	Tommy Irwin	1959 Thunderbird	$2,010
6	23	88	Jim Paschal	1959 Chevrolet	$1,460
7	1	3	Fireball Roberts	1959 Pontiac	$2,330
8	20	76	Larry Frank	1957 Chevrolet	$1,025
9	15	87	Buck Baker	1959 Chevrolet	$875
10	18	41	Jimmy Thompson	1959 Thunderbird	$805
11	28	64	Shep Langdon	1958 Ford	$600
12	25	27	Bill Champion	1957 Ford	$500
13	12	2	Joe Caspolich	1959 Oldsmobile	$470
14	3	22	Speedy Thompson	1959 Chevrolet	$565
15	29	16	Charlie Cregar	1959 Pontiac	$300
16	34	19	Herman Beam	1957 Chevrolet	$250
17	4	4	Rex White	1959 Chevrolet	$310
18	39	66	L.D. Austin	1957 Ford	$225
19	19	6	Cotton Owens	1959 Thunderbird	$600
20	9	42	Lee Petty	1959 Plymouth	$300
21	32	56	Bud Crothers	1957 Chevrolet	$150
22	47	35	Al White	1958 Ford	$150
23	31	34	G.C. Spencer	1957 Chevrolet	$150
24	30	13	Earl Balmer	1959 Chevrolet	$150
25	27	26	Dick Blackwell	1957 Ford	$150
26	24	20	Tiny Lund	1958 Ford	$150
27	33	30	Cale Yarborough	1958 Ford	$150
28	10	47	Jack Smith	1959 Chevrolet	$150
29	21	98	Marvin Panch	1959 Ford	$150
30	50	55	Johnny Patterson	1957 Chevrolet	$150
31	7	93	Banjo Matthews	1959 Thunderbird	$1,915
32	46	32	George Green	1958 Chevrolet	$150
33	35	9	Roy Tyner	1957 Chevrolet	$150
34	38	5	Bob Duell	1959 Ford	$150
35	11	49	Bob Welborn	1959 Chevrolet	$200
36	17	59	Tom Pistone	1959 Thunderbird	$325
37	41	91	Neil Castles	1957 Ford	$150
38	13	92	Possum Jones	1959 Thunderbird	$295
39	43	83	Lennie Page	1957 Ford	$150
40	40	95	Buddy Baker	1959 Ford	$150
41	42	23	Bob Perry	1959 Plymouth	$150
42	49	44	Joe Lee Johnson	1959 Chevrolet	$150
43	8	12	Joe Weatherly	1959 Thunderbird	$210
44	36	71	Dick Joslin	1957 Dodge	$150
45	2	10	Elmo Langley	1959 Buick	$180
46	26	61	Joe Eubanks	1958 Pontiac	$190
47	48	15	Marvin Porter	1957 Ford	$150
48	45	82	Elmo Henderson	1958 Ford	$150
49	44	86	Larry Flynn	1958 Ford	$150
50	37	14	Carl Burris	1957 Ford	$150

*was relieved by Joe Weatherly
**was relieved by Marvin Panch

Rebel 300 • May 14, 1960
Darlington Raceway, South Carolina

Finish	Start	No.	Driver	Car	Winnings
1	2	12	Joe Weatherly	1960 Ford	$9,250
2	7	43	Richard Petty	1960 Plymouth	$4,875
3	3	4	Rex White	1960 Chevrolet	$2,900
4	11	42	Lee Petty	1960 Plymouth	$1,940
5	31	87	Buck Baker	1960 Chevrolet	$1,500
6	10	93	Bobby Johns	1959 Thunderbird	$1,160
7	23	49	Bob Welborn	1960 Chevrolet	$925
8	14	85	Emanuel Zervakis	1960 Ford	$825
9	5	15	Tim Flock	1960 Ford	$700
10	15	77	Marvin Panch	1960 Ford	$600
11	28	39	Herb Tillman	1960 Chevrolet	$500
12	21	45	Joe Caspolich	1960 Oldsmobile	$400
13	4	5	Cotton Owens	1960 Pontiac	$350
14	19	78	Joe Lee Johnson	1960 Chevrolet	$400
15	25	48	G.C. Spencer	1958 Chevrolet	$250
16	9	11	Ned Jarrett	1960 Ford	$225
17	26	1	Buddy Baker	1960 Chevrolet	$200
18	16	76	Larry Frank	1959 Chevrolet	$200
19	8	26	Curtis Turner	1960 Ford	$200
20	1	22	Fireball Roberts	1960 Pontiac	$250
21	13	61	Jimmy Thompson	1959 Thunderbird	$200
22	6	69	Johnny Allen	1960 Chevrolet	$265
23	12	59	Tom Pistone	1960 Chevrolet	$265
24	17	26	Junior Johnson	1960 Chevrolet	$220
25	20	64	Bunkie Blackburn	1960 Ford	$200
26	22	9	Carl Burris	1960 Ford	$200
27	24	94	Banjo Matthews	1959 Thunderbird	$200
28	30	90	Runt Harris	1960 Chevrolet	$200
29	18	23	Doug Yates	1959 Plymouth	$200
30	27	86	Johnny Dollar	1958 Ford	$200
31	32	83	Curtis Crider	1958 Ford	$100
32	29	80	Neil Castles	1958 Ford	$200

Southern 500 • September 5, 1960
Darlington Raceway, South Carolina

Finish	Start	No.	Driver	Car	Winnings
1	2	47	Buck Baker	1960 Pontiac	$19,900
2	7	4	Rex White	1960 Chevrolet	$9,780
3	3	44	Jim Paschal	1960 Plymouth	$5,595
4	16	85	Emanuel Zervakis	1960 Chevrolet	$3,125
5	20	11	Ned Jarrett	1960 Ford	$2,000
6	8	43	Richard Petty	1960 Plymouth	$2,575
7	17	94	Banjo Matthews	1960 Ford	$1,255
8	21	73	Johnny Beauchamp	1960 Chevrolet	$1,025
9	1	22	Fireball Roberts	1960 Pontiac	$2,175
10	34	23	Doug Yates	1959 Plymouth	$775
11	24	77	Marvin Panch	1960 Ford	$700
12	26	70	Elmo Henderson	1958 Pontiac	$600
13	39	38	Clem Proctor	1960 Ford	$500
14	36	1	Paul Lewis	1960 Chevrolet	$450
15	29	81	Shorty Rollins	1960 Ford	$500
16	35	60	Jim Whitman	1960 Dodge	$350
17	41	74	L.D. Austin	1958 Chevrolet	$300
18	37	19	Herman Beam	1960 Ford	$250
19	32	45	Tiny Lund	1959 Olds	$250
20	43	83	Curtis Crider	1958 Ford	$250
21	4	12	Joe Weatherly	1960 Ford	$200
22	44	20	G.C. Spencer	1958 Ford	$200
23	25	61	Jimmy Thompson	1959 Thunderbird	$200
24	6	6	Cotton Owens	1960 Pontiac	$510
25	45	10	T.C. Hunt	1960 Plymouth	$200
26	30	99	Wilbur Rakestraw	1960 Ford	$200
27	22	67	David Pearson	1959 Chevrolet	$200
28	14	28	Fred Lorenzen	1960 Ford	$250
29	42	16	Steve McGrath	1959 Pontiac	$200
30	9	42	Lee Petty	1960 Plymouth	$470
31	33	39	Herb Tillman	1960 Chevrolet	$200
32	38	33	Reb Wickersham	1960 Oldsmobile	$200
33	46	54	Jimmy Pardue	1959 Dodge	$200
34	23	87	Buddy Baker	1960 Chevrolet	$200
35	47	96	Gene White	1960 Chevrolet	$200
36	28	7	Jim Reed	1960 Chevrolet	$200
37	13	69	Johnny Allen	1960 Chevrolet	$220
38	12	59	Tom Pistone	1960 Chevrolet	$230
39	19	90	Speedy Thompson	1960 Ford	$250
40	5	5	Bobby Johns	1960 Pontiac	$210
41	11	89	Joe Lee Johnson	1960 Chevrolet	$550
42	40	9	Roy Tyner	1959 Oldsmobile	$200
43	15	2	Possum Jones	1960 Chevrolet	$200
44	31	79	Johnny Miller	1960 Ford	$200
45	18	92	Elmo Langley	1959 Thunderbird	$220
46	27	64	Bunkie Blackburn	1960 Ford	$200
47	10	27	Junior Johnson	1960 Chevrolet	$200
48	48	35	E.J. Trivette	1959 Plymouth	$200

Rebel 300 • May 6, 1961
Darlington Raceway, South Carolina

Finish	Start	No.	Driver	Car	Winnings
1	1	28	Fred Lorenzen	1961 Ford	$8,420
2	8	21	Curtis Turner	1961 Ford	$4,600
3	9	69	Johnny Allen	1961 Chevrolet	$3,200
4	10	53	Bob Burdick	1961 Pontiac	$2,400
5	2	22	Fireball Roberts	1961 Pontiac	$1,665
6	17	3	Marvin Panch	1961 Pontiac	$1,050
7	6	6	Ralph Earnhardt	1961 Pontiac	$925
8	3	94	Banjo Matthews	1961 Ford	$865
9	5	72	Bobby Johns	1961 Ford	$700
10	11	11	Ned Jarrett	1961 Chevrolet	$650
11	7	29	Nelson Stacy	1961 Ford	$500
12	18	47	Larry Frank	1961 Pontiac	$400
13	14	85	Emanuel Zervakis	1961 Chevrolet	$370
14	22	54	Jimmy Pardue	1960 Chevrolet	$300
15	4	8	Joe Weatherly	1961 Pontiac	$250
16	26	00	Dave Mader	1961 Chevrolet	$275
17	20	48	G.C. Spencer	1960 Chevrolet	$200
18	21	2	Tommy Irwin	1960 Chevrolet	$200
19	25	82	Larry Flynn	1959 Chevrolet	$200
20	13	87	Buck Baker	1961 Chrysler	$565
21	28	68	Ed Livingston	1960 Ford	$200
22	32	62	Curtis Crider	1961 Mercury	$500
23	29	38	Ed Marsteller	1961 Ford	$200
24	12	4	Rex White	1961 Chevrolet	$340
25	15	86	Buddy Baker	1961 Chrysler	$200
26	24	55	Jimmy Thompson	1959 Thunderbird	$200
27	23	52	Tom Dill	1961 Ford	$230
28	19	1	Paul Lewis	1961 Chevrolet	$200
29	30	71	Bobby Waddell	1960 Dodge	$220
30	16	15	Tim Flock	1961 Ford	$200
31	27	61	Elmo Langley	1950 Thunderbird	$200
32	31	43	Richard Petty	1961 Plymouth	$200

Southern 500 • September 4, 1961
Darlington Raceway, South Carolina

Finish	Start	No.	Driver	Car	Winnings
1	3	29	Nelson Stacy	1961 Ford	$18,430
2	1	22	Fireball Roberts*	1961 Pontiac	$10,670
3	9	3	David Pearson	1961 Pontiac	$5,060
4	7	44	Jim Paschal	1961 Pontiac	$2,625
5	20	85	Emanuel Zervakis	1961 Chevrolet	$2,450
6	33	11	Ned Jarrett	1961 Chevrolet	$1,500
7	26	14	Johnny Allen	1961 Chevrolet	$1,195
8	18	24	Roscoe Thompson	1960 Pontiac	$1,195
9	6	6	Ralph Earnhardt	1961 Pontiac	$875
10	36	47	Rex White	1961 Pontiac	$925
11	12	72	Bobby Johns	1961 Ford	$750
12	16	66	Bill Morgan	1961 Ford	$700
13	32	30	Elmo Langley	1960 Chevrolet	$500
14	14	27	Junior Johnson	1961 Pontiac	$450
15	24	59	Tiny Lund	1961 Pontiac	$650
16	40	74	L.D. Austin	1961 Chevrolet	$350
17	35	54	Jimmy Pardue	1960 Chevrolet	$300
18	39	62	Curtis Crider	1961 Mercury	$750
19	23	19	Herman Beam	1960 Ford	$250
20	17	46	Larry Frank	1961 Pontiac	$480
21	25	90	Dave Mader	1961 Chevrolet	$280
22	4	8	Joe Weatherly	1961 Pontiac	$370
23	31	7	Jim Reed	1961 Chevrolet	$200
24	15	86	Buddy Baker	1961 Chrysler	$700
25	34	10	T.C. Hunt	1961 Dodge	$700
26	5	43	Richard Petty	1961 Plymouth	$1,110
27	11	87	Buck Baker	1961 Chrysler	$220
28	21	2	Tommy Irwin	1961 Chevrolet	$200
29	2	28	Fred Lorenzen	1961 Ford	$950
30	19	52	Cale Yarborough	1961 Ford	$200
31	8	42	Marvin Panch	1961 Plymouth	$200
32	28	82	Marvin Porter	1961 Ford	$200
33	29	1	Paul Lewis	1961 Chevrolet	$200
34	30	5	Woody Wilson	1961 Pontiac	$200
35	38	68	Ed Livingston	1961 Ford	$200
36	10	94	Banjo Matthews	1961 Ford	$430
37	22	32	Joe Caspolich	1961 Ford	$200
38	27	80	Darel Dieringer	1961 Ford	$300
39	13	9	Bunkie Blackburn	1961 Ford	$200
40	37	96	Friday Hassler	1960 Chevrolet	$200
41	43	99	George Alsobrook	1961 Ford	$200
42	41	75	Red Hollingsworth	1960 Chevrolet	$200
43	42	93	Lee Reitzel	1960 Ford	$200

*was relieved by Marvin Panch

Rebel 300 • May 12, 1962
Darlington Raceway, South Carolina

Finish	Start	No.	Driver	Car	Winnings
1	3	29	Nelson Stacy	1962 Ford	$7,900
2	5	21	Marvin Panch	1962 Ford	$4,890
3	1	28	Fred Lorenzen	1962 Ford	$3,400
4	11	47	Jack Smith*	1962 Pontiac	$2,270
5	14	6	Cotton Owens	1962 Pontiac	$1,765
6	32	66	Larry Frank	1962 Ford	$1,300
7	6	3	David Pearson	1962 Pontiac	$1,025
8	9	72	Bobby Johns	1962 Pontiac	$925
9	29	11	Ned Jarrett	1962 Chevrolet	$1,000
10	16	54	Jimmy Pardue	1962 Pontiac	$750
11	15	86	Buddy Baker	1962 Chrysler	$700
12	10	90	Darel Dieringer	1962 Dodge	$650
13	17	52	Cale Yarborough	1962 Ford	$600
14	12	87	Buck Baker	1962 Chrysler	$615
15	7	43	Richard Petty	1962 Plymouth	$500

Finish	Start	No.	Driver	Car	Winnings
16	22	68	Ed Livingston	1961 Ford	$450
17	26	1	George Green	1961 Chevrolet	$400
18	4	8	Joe Weatherly	1962 Pontiac	$370
19	25	80	Tubby Gonzales	1961 Ford	$300
20	27	60	Tom Cox	1960 Plymouth	$300
21	31	62	Curtis Crider	1962 Mercury	$200
22	19	2	Jim Paschal	1962 Pontiac	$200
23	28	93	Lee Reitzel	1962 Ford	$200
24	20	64	Elmo Langley	1962 Ford	$200
25	21	75	Ralph Earnhardt	1961 Pontiac	$200
26	18	77	Jim Reed	1962 Ford	$200
27	13	4	Rex White	1962 Chevrolet	$200
28	24	38	G.C. Spencer	1961 Ford	$200
29	23	20	Emanuel Zervakis	1962 Mercury	$200
30	30	97	Lee Roy Yarbrough	1962 Chevrolet	$200
31	8	39	Junior Johnson	1961 Pontiac	$200
32	2	22	Fireball Roberts	1962 Pontiac	$265

*was relieved by Johnny Allen

Southern 500 • September 3, 1962
Darlington Raceway, South Carolina

Finish	Start	No.	Driver	Car	Winnings
1	10	66	Larry Frank	1962 Ford	$21,730
2	2	3	Junior Johnson	1962 Pontiac	$10,155
3	8	21	Marvin Panch	1962 Ford	$5,150
4	7	6	David Pearson	1962 Pontiac	$3,325
5	6	43	Richard Petty	1962 Plymouth	$5,450
6	14	42	Jim Paschal	1962 Plymouth	$2,025
7	13	29	Nelson Stacy	1962 Ford	$1,525
8	19	11	Ned Jarrett	1962 Chevrolet	$1,575
9	18	4	Rex White	1962 Chevrolet	$1,355
10	5	8	Joe Weatherly	1962 Pontiac	$1,025
11	23	87	Buck Baker	1962 Chrysler	$950
12	12	54	Jimmy Pardue	1962 Pontiac	$900
13	16	20	Emanuel Zervakis	1962 Mercury	$800
14	28	49	Bob Welborn	1962 Pontiac	$700
15	31	61	Sherman Utsman	1962 Ford	$650
16	27	82	Elmo Langley	1961 Ford	$620
17	24	5	H.G. Rosier	1961 Pontiac	$550
18	42	97	Paul Lewis	1962 Chevrolet	$500
19	11	30	Tiny Lund	1962 Chevrolet	$470
20	34	84	Red Foote	1961 Ford	$450
21	33	1	George Green	1961 Chevrolet	$400
22	32	68	Ed Livingston	1961 Ford	$400
23	38	62	Curtis Crider	1962 Mercury	$400
24	3	28	Fred Lorenzen	1962 Ford	$730
25	39	19	Herman Beam	1961 Ford	$400
26	9	46	Johnny Allen	1962 Pontiac	$550
27	29	83	Lee Roy Yarbrough	1962 Pontiac	$400
28	22	48	G.C. Spencer	1962 Chevrolet	$400
29	37	96	T.C. Hunt	1961 Chevrolet	$400
30	15	26	Darel Dieringer	1962 Ford	$450
31	4	72	Bobby Johns	1962 Pontiac	$1,070
32	21	41	Bunkie Blackburn	1962 Plymouth	$400
33	36	93	Doc Reitzel	1962 Ford	$400
34	17	47	Jack Smith	1962 Pontiac	$550
35	30	36	Larry Thomas	1962 Dodge	$400
36	1	22	Fireball Roberts	1962 Pontiac	$1,030
37	20	86	Buddy Baker	1962 Chrysler	$400
38	25	92	Cale Yarborough	1962 Ford	$650
39	26	81	Roscoe Thompson	1962 Mercury	$530
40	41	79	Bill Champion	1962 Chevrolet	$400
41	35	18	Stick Elliott	1961 Pontiac	$400
42	40	91	Gary Sain	1962 Dodge	$400
43	43	2	Thomas Cox	1962 Pontiac	$400
44	44	38	Mat DeMatthews	1961 Ford	$400

Rebel 300 • May 11, 1963
Darlington Raceway, South Carolina

Finish	Start	No.	Driver	Car	Winnings
1	6	8	Joe Weatherly	1963 Pontiac	$11,100
2	5	22	Fireball Roberts	1963 Ford	$6,200
3	9	42	Richard Petty	1963 Plymouth	$4,980
4	2	21	Tiny Lund	1963 Ford	$2,665
5	10	7A	Bobby Johns	1963 Pontiac	$1,965
6	11	41	Jim Paschal	1963 Plymouth	$1,470
7	7	26	Darel Dieringer	1963 Mercury	$1,250
8	14	87	Buck Baker	1963 Pontiac	$1,000
9	16	54	Jimmy Pardue	1963 Ford	$850
10	18	5	Billy Wade	1963 Dodge	$650
11	22	52	Cale Yarborough	1962 Ford	$600
12	13	6	David Pearson	1963 Dodge	$600
13	21	16	G.C. Spencer	1963 Dodge	$500
14	24	73	Curtis Crider	1962 Pontiac	$450
15	19	47	Stick Elliott	1963 Pontiac	$400
16	20	71	Lee Roy Yarbrough	1963 Chevrolet	$420
17	8	24	Larry Frank	1963 Mercury	$350
18	29	09	Larry Manning	1962 Chevrolet	$300
19	27	56	Ed Livingston	1962 Ford	$300
20	15	11	Ned Jarrett	1963 Ford	$300
21	17	99	Bobby Isaac	1963 Ford	$390
22	23	27	Bob James	1963 Plymouth	$300
23	25	67	Reb Wickersham	1962 Pontiac	$300
24	26	19	Herman Beam	1962 Ford	$300
25	4	3	Junior Johnson	1963 Chevrolet	$1,300
26	28	86	Neil Castles	1963 Chrysler	$300
27	12	66	Johnny Allen	1963 Ford	$300
28	30	51	Bob Cooper	1962 Pontiac	$300
29	31	97	Possum Jones	1962 Chevrolet	$300
30	1	28	Fred Lorenzen	1963 Ford	$415
31	3	4	Rex White	1963 Chevrolet	$320

Southern 500 • September 2, 1963
Darlington Raceway, South Carolina

Finish	Start	No.	Driver	Car	Winnings
1	9	22	Fireball Roberts	1963 Ford	$22,150
2	6	21	Marvin Panch	1963 Ford	$12,650
3	1	28	Fred Lorenzen	1963 Ford	$6,550
4	7	29	Nelson Stacy	1963 Ford	$3,500
5	4	26	Darel Dieringer	1963 Mercury	$2,625
6	10	4	Rex White	1963 Mercury	$2,155
7	3	8	Joe Weatherly	1963 Mercury	$2,345
8	24	0	Tiny Lund	1963 Ford	$1,775
9	5	7	Bobby Johns	1963 Pontiac	$1,275
10	8	13	Buck Baker	1963 Chevrolet	$1,025
11	16	99	Bobby Isaac	1963 Ford	$950
12	18	43	Richard Petty*	1963 Plymouth	$1,030
13	22	70	Bunkie Blackburn	1962 Pontiac	$800
14	17	6	David Pearson	1963 Dodge	$950
15	20	54	Jimmy Pardue	1963 Ford	$650
16	27	62	Curtis Crider	1963 Mercury	$600
17	21	19	Cale Yarborough	1963 Ford	$500
18	35	09	Elmo Langley	1962 Chevrolet	$500
19	28	60	Bud Harless	1962 Pontiac	$500
20	2	3	Junior Johnson	1963 Chevrolet	$4,705
21	11	11	Ned Jarrett	1963 Ford	$570
22	14	41	Jim Paschal	1963 Plymouth	$500
23	19	87	Buddy Baker	1963 Pontiac	$570
24	12	47	G.C. Spencer	1963 Plymouth	$500
25	26	17	Ralph Earnhardt	1962 Pontiac	$570
26	29	23	H.G. Rosier	1962 Plymouth	$500
27	15	42	Bob James	1963 Plymouth	$500
28	13	5	Billy Wade	1963 Dodge	$500
29	25	92	Lee Roy Yarbrough	1963 Ford	$630

Finish	Start	No.	Driver	Car	Winnings
30	23	36	Larry Thomas	1962 Dodge	$500
31	34	9	Roy Tyner	1962 Chevrolet	$500
32	30	76	Larry Manning	1961 Ford	$500
33	32	57	Bobby Keck	1963 Ford	$500
34	31	86	Neil Castles	1962 Chevrolet	$500
35	36	2	Bob Welborn	1962 Pontiac	$500
36	39	05	Possum Jones	1961 Pontiac	$500
37	37	53	Paul Lewis	1963 Ford	$500
38	40	68	Frank Graham	1961 Ford	$500
39	41	56	Ed Livingston	1962 Ford	$500
40	38	93	Lee Reitzel	1962 Ford	$500
41	33	20	Emmanuel Zervakis	1963 Ford	$500

*Jim Paschal relieved Richard Petty

Rebel 300 • May 9, 1964
Darlington Raceway, South Carolina

Finish	Start	No.	Driver	Car	Winnings
1	1	28	Fred Lorenzen	1964 Ford	$10,265
2	5	22	Fireball Roberts	1964 Ford	$5,990
3	4	27	Junior Johnson	1964 Ford	$4,510
4	10	11	Ned Jarrett	1964 Ford	$2,995
5	3	54	Jimmy Pardue	1964 Plymouth	$2,100
6	6	6	David Pearson	1964 Dodge	$1,500
7	18	1	Billy Wade	1964 Mercury	$1,270
8	14	03	Lee Roy Yarbrough	1964 Dodge	$1,000
9	20	25	Paul Goldsmith	1964 Plymouth	$900
10	2	43	Richard Petty	1964 Plymouth	$840
11	8	21	Marvin Panch	1964 Ford	$750
12	7	41	Jim Paschal	1964 Plymouth	$700
13	12	16	Johnny Allen	1964 Mercury	$650
14	13	5	Larry Thomas	1964 Dodge	$600
15	22	82	Bunkie Blackburn	1963 Pontiac	$550
16	16	49	G.C. Spencer	1964 Chevrolet	$500
17	24	56	J.T. Putney	1962 Chevrolet	$450
18	25	95	Ken Spikes	1964 Plymouth	$400
19	15	19	Cale Yarborough	1964 Ford	$350
20	21	89	Tiny Lund	1964 Plymouth	$300
21	9	4	Rex White	1964 Mercury	$415
22	27	52	E.J. Trivette	1962 Chevrolet	$300
23	23	60	Bob Cooper	1963 Ford	$300
24	24	09	Roy Mayne	1962 Chevrolet	$300
25	17	14	Darel Dieringer	1964 Mercury	$415
26	11	3	Buck Baker	1964 Dodge	$340
27	19	26	Bobby Isaac	1964 Dodge	$340
28	26	01	Curtis Crider	1963 Mercury	$300
29	25	87	Buddy Baker	1963 Dodge	$300
30	28	88	Neil Castles	1962 Chrysler	$300
31	31	78	Buddy Arrington	1962 Dodge	$300
32	32	86	Jimmy Helms	1962 Chrysler	$300

Southern 500 • September 7, 1964
Darlington Raceway, South Carolina

Finish	Start	No.	Driver	Car	Winnings
1	6	3	Buck Baker	1964 Dodge	$21,230
2	4	41	Jim Paschal	1964 Plymouth	$8,960
3	1	43	Richard Petty	1964 Plymouth	$8,170
4	16	11	Ned Jarrett	1964 Ford	$3,575
5	5	54	Jimmy Pardue	1964 Plymouth	$2,955
6	17	1	Billy Wade	1964 Mercury	$2,375
7	22	19	Larry Thomas	1964 Ford	$1,775
8	14	06	Cale Yarborough	1964 Ford	$1,525
9	27	46	J.T. Putney	1963 Chevrolet	$1,345
10	38	53	Bob Cooper	1963 Ford	$1,025
11	36	02	Curtis Crider	1963 Mercury	$950
12	2	6	David Pearson	1964 Dodge	$1,130
13	27	48	Bobby Keck	1963 Ford	$850
14	41	9	Roy Tyner	1964 Chevrolet	$800
15	32	36	Major Melton	1963 Dodge	$750
16	30	09	Roy Mayne	1962 Chevrolet	$700
17	11	03	Lee Roy Yarbrough	1964 Dodge	$720
18	15	49	G.C. Spencer	1964 Ford	$600
19	33	71	Sam McQuagg	1963 Ford	$550
20	10	26	Bobby Isaac	1964 Dodge	$530
21	23	64	Elmo Langley	1964 Ford	$500
22	3	28	Fred Lorenzen	1964 Ford	$620
23	12	27	Junior Johnson	1964 Ford	$610
24	7	16	Darel Dieringer	1964 Mercury	$600
25	24	45	Bud Moore	1963 Plymouth	$500
26	29	04	H.B. Bailey	1964 Pontiac	$500
27	18	7	Bobby Johns	1964 Ford	$500
28	9	25	Paul Goldmith	1964 Plymouth	$790
29	19	76	Larry Frank	1964 Ford	$620
30	21	82	Bunkie Blackburn	1964 Pontiac	$600
31	20	10	Buddy Baker	1964 Ford	$500
32	18	5	Earl Balmer	1964 Dodge	$580
33	25	55	Tiny Lund	1964 Ford	$750
34	39	58	Doug Moore	1964 Chevrolet	$500
35	35	86	Neil Castles	1962 Chrysler	$500
36	31	42	Bill McMahan	1963 Pontiac	$500
37	26	60	Doug Cooper	1964 Ford	$630
38	28	63	Don Hume	1963 Ford	$500
39	13	21	Nelson Stacy	1964 Ford	$500
40	34	52	E.J. Trivette	1962 Chevrolet	$500
41	44	13	Bud Harless	1964 Ford	$500
42	40	88	Jimmy Helms	1962 Chrysler	$500
43	43	01	Ed Livingston	1963 Mercury	$500
44	42	0	Frank Graham	1962 Ford	$500

Rebel 300 • May 8, 1965
Darlington Raceway, South Carolina

Finish	Start	No.	Driver	Car	Winnings
1	3	26	Junior Johnson	1965 Ford	$10,490
2	6	16	Darel Dieringer	1964 Mercury	$6,155
3	5	11	Ned Jarrett	1965 Ford	$4,460
4	4	29	Dick Hutcherson	1965 Ford	$2,925
5	9	7	Bobby Johns	1965 Ford	$1,100
6	14	88	Buddy Baker	1964 Dodge	$1,500
7	11	24	Sam McQuagg	1965 Ford	$1,250
8	26	55	Tiny Lund	1964 Ford	$1,000
9	10	49	G.C. Spencer	1964 Ford	$900
10	27	87	Buck Baker	1965 Chevrolet	$800
11	2	21	Marvin Panch	1965 Ford	$770
12	20	52	E.J. Trivette	1963 Chevrolet	$700
13	16	86	Neil Castles	1965 Dodge	$650
14	30	35	Doug Cooper	1964 Dodge	$600
15	18	34	Wendell Scott	1963 Ford	$550
16	25	41	Jim Paschal	1965 Chevrolet	$500
17	22	68	Bob Derrington	1963 Ford	$450
18	21	53	Jimmy Helms	1963 Ford	$400
19	19	44	Larry Hess	1964 Ford	$350
20	15	37	Bub Strickler	1964 Ford	$300
21	13	90	Sonny Hutchins	1964 Ford	$350
22	28	14	Bunkie Blackburn	1965 Plymouth	$300
23	12	0	J.T. Putney	1965 Chevrolet	$300
24	29	10	Cale Yarborough	1964 Ford	$300
25	1	28	Fred Lorenzen	1965 Ford	$415
26	31	59	Tom Pistone	1964 Ford	$300
27	8	76	Larry Frank	1964 Ford	$340
28	23	9	Roy Tyner	1964 Chevrolet	$300
29	17	17	Junior Spencer	1964 Ford	$300
30	7	15	Earl Balmer	1964 Mercury	$320
31	24	38	Wayne Smith	1965 Chevrolet	$300

Southern 500 • September 6, 1965
Darlington Raceway, South Carolina

Finish	Start	No.	Driver	Car	Winnings
1	10	11	Ned Jarrett	1965 Ford	$21,060
2	14	86	Buck Baker*	1965 Plymouth	$9,170
3	5	16	Darel Dieringer	1964 Mercury	$7,200
4	33	46	Roy Mayne	1965 Chevrolet	$3,225
5	24	67	Buddy Arrington	1964 Dodge	$2,400
6	22	04	H.B. Bailey	1964 Pontiac	$1,750
7	31	18	Stick Elliott	1965 Chevrolet	$1,500
8	41	79	Frank Warren	1963 Chevrolet	$1,250
9	19	19	J.T. Putney	1965 Chevrolet	$1,000
10	44	57	Wendell Scott	1964 Ford	$900
11	2	28	Fred Lorenzen	1965 Ford	$1,550
12	37	53	Jimmy Helms	1963 Ford	$800
13	42	68	Bob Derrington	1963 Ford	$775
14	18	1	Paul Lewis	1964 Ford	$750
15	39	38	Wayne Smith	1965 Chevrolet	$725
16	40	52	E.J. Trivette	1963 Chevrolet	$700
17	16	7	Bobby Johns	1964 Pontiac	$695
18	32	63	Don Hume	1963 Ford	$650
19	6	29	Dick Hutcherson	1965 Ford	$625
20	20	49	G.C. Spencer	1964 Ford	$620
21	35	44	Larry Hess	1964 Ford	$615
22	7	41	Jim Paschal	1965 Chevrolet	$710
23	34	07	Bud Harless	1964 Ford	$605
24	38	75	Gene Black	1964 Ford	$600
25	30	72	Neil Castles	1964 Ford	$595
26	15	64	Elmo Langley	1964 Ford	$590
27	25	3	Lee Roy Yarbrough	1965 Chevrolet	$635
28	17	87	Buddy Baker	1965 Chevrolet	$580
29	11	24	Sam McQuagg	1965 Ford	$1,015
30	9	27	Cale Yarborough	1965 Ford	$830
31	12	33	Bunkie Blackburn	1965 Chevrolet	$695
32	4	15	Earl Balmer	1964 Mercury	$580
33	29	62	Doug Cooper	1965 Chevrolet	$555
34	13	17	Junior Spencer	1964 Ford	$620
35	8	14	Curtis Turner	1965 Plymouth	$545
36	27	4	Bobby Wawak	1964 Mercury	$560
37	3	21	Marvin Panch	1965 Ford	$605
38	43	97	Henley Gray	1964 Ford	$530
39	26	55	Tiny Lund	1964 Ford	$555
40	28	25	Bud Moore	1964 Ford	$520
41	36	00	Burt Robbins	1964 Ford	$515
42	21	23	Buren Skeen	1964 Ford	$510
43	23	03	Reb Wickersham	1965 Ford	$505
44	1	26	Junior Johnson	1965 Ford	$750

*was relieved by Buddy Baker

Rebel 400 • April 30, 1966
Darlington Raceway, South Carolina

Finish	Start	No.	Driver	Car	Winnings
1	1	43	Richard Petty	1966 Plymouth	$12,115
2	7	99	Paul Goldsmith	1965 Plymouth	$6,570
3	11	6	David Pearson	1965 Dodge	$4,145
4	9	3	Bunkie Blackburn	1965 Dodge	$2,225
5	10	49	G.C. Spencer	1965 Plymouth	$1,670
6	5	14	Jim Paschal	1966 Plymouth	$1,250
7	15	64	Elmo Langley	1964 Ford	$1,000
8	26	87	Buck Baker	1966 Oldsmobile	$900
9	17	48	James Hylton	1965 Dodge	$965
10	12	1	Paul Lewis	1965 Plymouth	$840
11	23	4	John Sears	1964 Ford	$750
12	14	29	J.T. Putney	1966 Chevrolet	$725
13	28	97	Henley Gray	1966 Ford	$700
14	36	86	Neil Castles	1965 Plymouth	$675
15	30	77	Joel Davis	1965 Plymouth	$650

Finish	Start	No.	Driver	Car	Winnings
16	19	24	Bobby Allison	1966 Ford	$645
17	13	7	Bobby Johns	1966 Chevrolet	$600
18	16	18	Stick Elliott	1966 Chevrolet	$575
19	25	46	Roy Mayne	1966 Chevrolet	$550
20	29	30	Walter Ballard	1964 Ford	$525
21	24	88	Buddy Baker	1966 Chevrolet	$500
22	2	16	Darel Dieringer	1966 Mercury	$490
23	3	71	Earl Balmer	1965 Dodge	$520
24	33	74	Gene Black	1964 Ford	$470
25	8	22	Curtis Turner	1965 Chevrolet	$460
26	34	25	Wendell Scott	1965 Ford	$450
27	22	67	Buddy Arrington	1964 Dodge	$445
28	31	38	Wayne Smith	1966 Chevrolet	$440
29	4	12	Lee Roy Yarbrough	1966 Dodge	$445
30	6	98	Sam McQuagg	1966 Dodge	$430
31	21	55	Tiny Lund	1964 Ford	$425
32	18	02	Doug Cooper	1965 Plymouth	$460
33	35	9	Roy Tyner	1966 Chevrolet	$415
34	20	59	Tom Pistone	1964 Ford	$410
35	27	66	Wayne Woodward	1966 Chevrolet	$405
36	32	96	Sonny Lamphear	1964 Ford	$400

Southern 500 • September 5, 1966
Darlington Raceway, South Carolina

Finish	Start	No.	Driver	Car	Winnings
1	3	16	Darel Dieringer	1966 Mercury	$20,900
2	2	43	Richard Petty	1966 Plymouth	$8,975
3	13	6	David Pearson	1966 Dodge	$4,700
4	14	42	Marvin Panch	1966 Plymouth	$2,775
5	9	28	Fred Lorenzen	1966 Ford	$2,300
6	11	14	Jim Paschal	1966 Plymouth	$2,595
7	10	29	Dick Hutcherson	1965 Ford	$1,280
8	1	12	Lee Roy Yarbrough	1966 Dodge	$1,650
9	5	98	Sam McQuagg	1966 Dodge	$900
10	18	49	G.C. Spencer	1966 Plymouth	$1,180
11	7	21	Cale Yarborough	1966 Ford	$700
12	21	1	Paul Lewis	1965 Plymouth	$925
13	20	11	Ned Jarrett	1966 Ford	$1,375
14	12	26	Curtis Turner	1966 Ford	$600
15	16	48	James Hylton	1965 Dodge	$800
16	4	99	Paul Goldsmith	1966 Plymouth	$605
17	19	36	H.B. Bailey	1966 Pontiac	$840
18	23	64	Elmo Langley	1964 Ford	$710
19	25	19	J.T. Putney	1966 Chevrolet	$725
20	40	4	John Sears	1964 Ford	$695
21	44	44	Larry Hess	1964 Ford	$665
22	38	97	Henley Gray	1966 Ford	$660
23	36	88	Neil Castles	1966 Chevrolet	$655
24	43	34	Wendell Scott	1965 Ford	$650
25	37	72	Bill Champion	1964 Ford	$645
26	30	79	Frank Warren	1964 Chevrolet	$590
27	26	20	Bunkie Blackburn	1964 Mercury	$615
28	24	24	Tiny Lund	1966 Ford	$580
29	28	09	Friday Hassler	1966 Chevrolet	$575
30	6	71	Earl Balmer	1965 Dodge	$470
31	31	93	Blackie Watt	1964 Ford	$465
32	42	75	Earl Brooks	1966 Ford	$510
33	8	3	Buddy Baker	1965 Dodge	$455
34	32	89	Eddie MacDonald	1965 Chevrolet	$450
35	22	47	Stick Elliott	1966 Chevrolet	$445

Finish	Start	No.	Driver	Car	Winnings
36	33	2	Bobby Allison	1965 Chevrolet	$640
37	17	7	Bobby Johns	1966 Chevrolet	$535
38	39	51	Bob Derrington	1965 Chevrolet	$480
39	29	67	Buddy Arrington	1965 Dodge	$425
40	34	38	Wayne Smith	1966 Chevrolet	$520
41	27	87	Buck Baker	1966 Oldsmobile	$435
42	35	25	Doug Cooper	1964 Ford	$460
43	15	04	Jerry Grant	1965 Plymouth	$405
44	41	73	Jimmy Helms	1964 Ford	$450

Rebel 400 • May 13, 1967
Darlington Raceway, South Carolina

Finish	Start	No.	Driver	Car	Winnings
1	2	43	Richard Petty	1967 Plymouth	$14,090
2	1	17	David Pearson	1967 Ford	$8,285
3	9	29	Dick Hutcherson	1967 Ford	$5,005
4	11	6	Bobby Allison	1967 Dodge	$2,775
5	8	16	Sam McQuagg	1967 Mercury	$2,175
6	13	1	Paul Lewis	1967 Dodge	$1,650
7	6	99	Paul Goldsmith	1967 Plymouth	$1,350
8	10	37	Bobby Isaac	1965 Dodge	$1,240
9	23	64	Elmo Langley	1966 Ford	$1,125
10	29	38	Wayne Smith	1966 Chevrolet	$1,050
11	25	10	Bill Champion	1966 Ford	$975
12	31	34	Wendell Scott	1965 Ford	$925
13	28	45	Don Biederman	1965 Ford	$900
14	7	14	Jim Paschal	1967 Plymouth	$875
15	19	05	Armond Holley	1966 Chevrolet	$850
16	35	20	Clyde Lynn	1966 Ford	$800
17	36	09	Neil Castles	1966 Chevrolet	$775
18	21	4	John Sears	1966 Ford	$750
19	12	48	James Hylton	1965 Dodge	$720
20	30	18	Dick Johnson	1967 Ford	$675
21	33	97	Henley Gray	1966 Ford	$650
22	3	21	Earl Balmer	1967 Ford	$625
23	32	63	Larry Manning	1966 Ford	$600
24	4	3	Buddy Baker	1967 Dodge	$610
25	27	80	Gary Sain	1967 Ford	$575
26	34	62	Ken Spikes	1967 Pontiac	$560
27	15	2	Donnie Allison	1965 Chevrolet	$550
28	26	67	Buddy Arrington	1965 Dodge	$540
29	17	49	G.C. Spencer	1967 Plymouth	$650
30	5	26	Darel Dieringer	1967 Ford	$530
31	16	87	Buck Baker	1966 Ford	$525
32	14	39	Friday Hassler	1966 Chevrolet	$525
33	18	11	J.T. Putney	1966 Chevrolet	$555
34	20	79	Frank Warren	1966 Chevrolet	$510
35	22	46	Roy Mayne	1966 Chevrolet	$525
36	24	25	Jabe Thomas	1967 Ford	$500

Southern 500 • September 4, 1967
Darlington Raceway, South Carolina

Finish	Start	No.	Driver	Car	Winnings
1	1	43	Richard Petty	1967 Plymouth	$26,900
2	11	17	David Pearson*	1967 Ford	$10,825
3	4	42	G.C. Spencer	1967 Plymouth	$6,175
4	10	72	Charlie Glotzbach	1967 Dodge	$3,325
5	12	53	Bud Moore	1967 Dodge	$2,725
6	14	71	Bobby Isaac	1967 Dodge	$1,800
7	6	12	Donnie Allison	1967 Ford	$1,650

Finish	Start	No.	Driver	Car	Winnings
8	15	48	James Hylton	1965 Dodge	$1,500
9	13	14	Jim Paschal	1967 Plymouth	$1,400
10	28	79	Frank Warren	1966 Chevrolet	$1,300
11	18	4	John Sears	1966 Ford	$1,250
12	33	06	Neil Castles	1965 Dodge	$1,350
13	25	59	Roy Mayne	1966 Chevrolet	$1,175
14	27	76	Earl Brooks	1966 Ford	$1,075
15	30	67	Buddy Arrington	1965 Dodge	$1,000
16	16	7	Bobby Johns	1966 Chevrolet	$950
17	38	19	E.J. Trivette	1966 Ford	$950
18	39	45	Bill Seifert	1965 Ford	$900
19	36	97	Henley Gray	1966 Ford	$850
20	42	94	Don Biederman	1966 Chevrolet	$825
21	44	9	Ken Spikes	1966 Chevrolet	$800
22	29	34	Wendell Scott	1966 Ford	$725
23	34	11	J.T. Putney	1966 Chevrolet	$700
24	17	26	Darel Dieringer	1967 Ford	$750
25	22	87	Doug Cooper	1966 Ford	$650
26	5	99	Paul Goldsmith	1967 Plymouth	$640
27	43	01	Dr. Don Tarr	1967 Ford	$680
28	24	10	Bill Champion	1966 Ford	$720
29	32	24	Bobby Mausgrover	1967 Ford	$610
30	2	3	Buddy Baker	1967 Dodge	$675
31	21	36	H.B. Bailey	1966 Pontiac	$590
32	19	2	Bobby Allison	1965 Chevrolet	$605
33	26	38	Wayne Smith	1966 Chevrolet	$620
34	23	64	Elmo Langley	1966 Ford	$560
35	3	6	Sam McQuagg	1967 Dodge	$580
36	7	29	Dick Hutcherson	1967 Ford	$550
37	37	20	Clyde Lynn	1966 Ford	$590
38	35	62	Roy Tyner	1967 Pontiac	$580
39	8	16	Lee Roy Yarbrough	1967 Mercury	$525
40	20	55	Tiny Lund	1966 Ford	$520
41	41	75	Bob Cooper	1966 Ford	$565
42	31	25	Jabe Thomas	1967 Ford	$510
43	40	31	Ed Negre	1966 Ford	$555
44	9	21	Cale Yarborough	1967 Ford	$620

*was relieved by Cale Yarborough

Grand National Champions

Year	Champion
1950	Bill Rexford
1951	Herb Thomas
1952	Tim Flock
1953	Herb Thomas
1954	Lee Petty
1955	Tim Flock
1956	Buck Baker
1957	Buck Baker
1958	Lee Petty
1959	Lee Petty
1960	Rex White
1961	Ned Jarrett
1962	Joe Weatherly
1963	Joe Weatherly
1964	Richard Petty
1965	Ned Jarrett
1966	David Pearson
1967	Richard Petty

Index

"Lady in Black, The" 6, 25, 73, 141, 146, 150
AAA Speedway Car Race, 47
Agobashian, Freddie, 103
Allen, Johnny, 99, 113
Allison, Bobby, 135, 147
Allison, Donnie, 147
Arness, James, 73
Ayulo Manuel, 47, 59
Baker Jr., Elzie Wylie "Buddy" 87, 90, 131, 145, 147
Baker, Cannonball, 83
Baker, Elzie Wylie "Buck" 14, 15, 19, 37, 25, 41, 45, 51, 101, 126, 131, 133, 145–147
Balmer, Earl, 142
Beam, Herman, 130
Beauchamp, Johnny, 11, 42
Becker, Lester, 115
Beithelete, Gene, 130
Benson, Jr., Paul, 19, 51, 71, 111, 123
Bentley, Roy, 58
Blackburn, Bunkis, 98
Brain, George, 15, 44, 115
Brasington, Harold 17, 21, 25, 51, 141, 150
Brunnemer, Mary Ann, 108
Bryan, Beth, 149
Bryant, Grover, 64
Burdick, Bob, 19, 87, 90, 92, 96
Burdick, Roy, 87, 90
Burrie, Carl, 98
Byron, Red, 34, 37, 127
Campbell, Wally, 26
Carolina, Wylie, 97
Caspolich, Joe, 19, 69, 92, 96
Castles, Neil, 130
Catlin, Russ, 14, 15, 72, 87, 90, 103, 113, 117, 126, 127, 133
Chestnut, Martha Dean, 41
Clement, Louis and Crawford, 130
Colvin, Robert E. "Bob" 51, 64, 83, 100, 115, 119, 125, 133, 142, 145
Comstock, Gene, 45
Connell, Lee, 34
Cooper, Bob, 125
Cooper, Doug, 137
Craft, John, 42
Crawford, Walt, 26
Curtis, Ken, 135
Darlington Films, Inc., 115
Darlington International Raceway (Darlington Raceway), 9, 15, 17, 20, 25, 59, 64, 65, 71, 91
Darlington Pure Record Club, 130
Darlington Raceway Radio Network (WJMX), 19, 51, 66, 87, 111, 123,
Daytona 500, 10, 17, 21, 42, 145, 150
Dieringer, Darel, 113, 128, 137, 138, 145
Dove, Fred, 43
Eargle, Pops, 130
Earnhardt, Dale, 67
Eubanks, Joe, 15, 38, 42,76, 79, 96
Fabulous Hudson Hornet, 37
Faircloth, Rudy, 15
Faulkner, Walt, 59
Fielden, Greg, 47
Fielden, Larry, 43
Fire-resistant coverall, 47
Flock, Thuman Fontell "Fonty" 29, 37, 39, 42–44, 53, 57, 58, 61, 65, 69, 67–69
Flock, Tim, 38, 52, 57, 61
Florida Jalousie, 48
Foote, Red, 112
Foster, Jim, 96

Fox, Ray, 130
France Sr., Bill, 17, 21, 25, 31, 47, 61, 65
Frank, Larry, 112, 113
Frank, Larry, 116, 117, 130, 145
Frank, Mundy, 31
Goldsmith, Paul, 57, 61, 63, 67–69, 128, 146
Gowen, Matt, 43
Grand National Division, 13, 37, 38, 48, 49, 104
Gray, Eddie, 76
Hanna, Pat, 126
Hard Drivin' 19, 87
Helmets, racing, 47
Hoffa, Jimmy, 141
Holman, John, 71, 111, 130
Hudson Hornet, 42
Hunt, T. C., 107
Hunter, Don, 17
Hunter, Jim, 18, 73, 145, 150
Hutcherson, Dick, 135, 146, 147
Hylton, James, 147
Indianapolis 500, 10, 20, 21
International Speedway Corporation, 19, 150
Isaac, Bobby, 23, 128, 147
James, Bob, 121
Jarrett, Martha, 135
Jarrett, Ned, 104, 111, 135, 145
Joe Weatherly Stock Car Museum, 19, 127, 133, 150
Johns, Bobby, 87, 90, 97, 121, 128, 130, 137
Johns, Shorty, 87, 90
Johnson, Junior, 41, 113, 116, 117, 130, 141
Johnson, Vickie, 135
Joslyn, Dick, 19, 96
Kelkhaefer, Carl, 52, 53, 58
Kelly, Godwin, 17
Kimberling, Don, 75
Kirkland, Tom, 51, 63, 113, 129, 142, 145, 147
Kite, Harold, 26
Langley, Elmo, 19, 92, 93, 96, 112, 129, 147
Lawing, Houston A., 130
Lewallen, Jimmy, 15, 38
Lilly, Betty, 135
Little Reb 119, 125
Long, Bondy, 130
Lorenson, Fred, 22, 105, 111, 122, 125, 134, 145
Louise, Winkie, 149
Lund, Tiny, 119, 122, 147
Mahoney, Chuck, 29
Mantz, Johnny, 19, 29
Martin, Pee Wee, 29
Matthews, Banjo, 37, 91, 92
Matz, Johnny, 17
McDuffie, Paul, 97, 133
McGriff, Hershell, 28, 29, 44
McQuagg, Sam, 135, 138, 147
Melton, Major, 125
Melton, Ray, 95
Mills, Thomas (Curly), 147
Mills, Wayne, 135
Modifieds, 41, 43, 48
Moody, Ralph, 48, 71, 111, 130
Moore, Bud, 18, 96, 130, 133, 150
Moriarty, Frank, 42
Motor Racing Network (MRN), 19, 123
Mundy, Frank, 37
Myers, Billy, 64
Myers, Bobby, 65, 68, 69
Myers, Chocolate, 67
Myler, Ken (Red), 130
Nab, Herb, 130

NASCAR Grand National Division, 18, 38, 52, 59, 63, 73, 101, 146, 150
National Association of Stock Car Auto Racing (NASCAR), 9, 13, 14, 17, 21, 25, 28, 31, 37, 41, 42, 48, 51, 57, 65, 66, 71, 76, 85, 87, 90, 95–97, 100, 101, 103, 104, 108, 111, 113, 116, 117, 119, 125, 126, 134, 141, 145, 150,
Nichels, Ray, 130, 135
O'Connor, Pat, 59
Osborne, Roy, 130
Owens, Cotton, 67, 71, 90, 130
Pagan, Eddie, 72, 73, 76, 84
Panch, Marvin, 19, 61, 71, 91, 96
Paperhanger's Special: City of Florence, 92
Parrish, George, 68
Parsons, Johnnie, 59
Paschal, Jim, 126, 146, 147
Paterson, Johnny, 37
Patterson, Kimmy, 123
Pearce, Al, 17
Pearson, David, 104, 106, 126, 130, 147
PeeDee 200, 59
Petty, Lee, 11, 12, 37, 42, 67, 69, 87, 90, 92, 96, 112, 145
Petty, Richard, 19, 20, 73, 87, 91, 92, 96, 112, 125, 126, 141, 142, 149,
Pistone, Tom, 111, 135, 147
Pointevint, Ginger, 116
Price, Tom, 15
Pure Oil Company, 15, 44, 47, 115, 122, 133,
Pure Record Club, 19, 96
Ramsey, Sherman, 17
Rathmann, Dick, 37, 38, 42, 43
Reb, Johnny, 123
Rebel 300, 13, 18, 63, 64, 87, 89, 90, 91, 95, 96, 99–101, 111, 119, 121, 125, 127, 130, 133, 134, 137, 141, 150
Rebel 400, 18, 97, 141, 149, 150,
Reed, Jim, 19, 57, 61, 87, 93, 104, 133
Rexford, Bill, 29
Riggs, Randy, 17
Roberts Jr., Edward Glenn "Fireball" 19, 47–49, 51, 58, 71, 76, 83, 85, 87, 92, 93, 96, 101, 105, 111, 119, 121, 123, 125, 126, 127, 133, 134,
Roberts, Doris, 83
Rockingham, 145
Roll bar, 41, 63
Roll cage, 41
Rookie of the Year, 104
Rosier, H. G., 114
Rudeen, Kenneth, 72
Russo-Nichels Special, 59
Schipman, Scrunt, 92
Schmidt Special, 59
Schuyler, Bobby, 130
Scorebrain, 104
Scott, Wendell, 135, 147
Sellers, Sherri, 131
Setzer, Ned, 135
Shorty, York, 33
Shuman, Buddy, 33, 45
Skeen, Buren, 135
Skeleton, Betty, 57, 61
Slicks 146
Smith, Bob, 26
Smith, Bruton, 141
Smith, Jack, 76, 83, 96, 101, 112
Smith, Louise, 25, 25
Sosebee, Cober, 15, 25, 43
Southern 400, 123

Southern 500, 9, 13, 14, 17, 19, 20, 21, 23, 25, 31, 34, 35, 37, 38, 41, 43, 47, 48, 49, 51, 53–55, 57, 58, 63, 64, 66, 67, 69, 71, 72, 83, 85, 87, 90–93, 95, 96, 101, 105, 108, 111–117, 119, 125–128, 131, 133, 135, 142, 145–147, 149, 150,
Speedway Division, 37, 41
Spencer, G. C., 130
Sportsman Division, 37
Stacy, Nelson, 108
Stock Car Racing's Father of the Year award, 115
Stock car, 13
Stock car, modified, 13
Stone, Milburn, 135
Strictly stock class, 47, 48
Stroppe, Bill, 130
Sullivan, Jack, 130
Sutton, Pat, 25
Suzuka Thunder Special 100, 93
Sweatlund, Charles, 97
Talbert, Bob, 95
Taylor, Jesse James, 33
Taylor, Joe, 97
Teague, Marshall, 31
Teamsters union, 141
Thomas, Herb, 31, 33, 35, 35, 47, 49, 51, 54, 55, 67, 68
Thompson, Dick, 141
Thompson, Eldridge, 95
Thompson, Jimmy, 25
Thompson, Johnny, 59
Thompson, Roscoe, 106
Thompson, Speedy, 14, 19, 51, 61, 69, 92, 93, 96
Thompson, Tommy, 35
Thumond, Strom, 25
Thunder in Carolina, 19
Turner, Curtis, 25, 57, 63, 67, 69, 71, 76, 83, 87, 88, 89, 103, 133, 141, 145, 147,
Tyler, Red, 92
Tyner, Roy, 97
Utsman, Sherman, 112
Van Witzenburg, Bob, 123, 123
Vaughan, Linda, 122
Wallace, Barney, 141, 145
Wanderer, John, 130
Wantin, Sadie B., 19
Weatherly, Bob, 43
Weatherly, Joe, 18, 63, 64, 69, 73, 76, 85, 87, 92, 95, 100, 101, 103, 104, 111, 113, 125, 133, 134, 141, 150
Webner, Tony, 111
Welborn, Bob, 57, 61, 92, 98
Westmoreland, Hubert, 133
Wheeler, Humpy, 96
White, Rex, 73, 92, 113
Wickersham, Reb, 135
Widenhouse, Dink, 58
Williamson, Robin, 57
Windham, Allen, 92
Winston Cup Series, 13, 37, 93, 146, 150
Wood, Glen, 130, 147
Wood, Leonard, 130
World 600, 125
World War II, 47
Yarborough, Cale, 66, 114, 117, 119, 125, 135, 138, 139. 147
Yarborough, Lee Roy, 126, 138, 139
Yates, Doug, 135
Yunick, Henry (Smokey), 61, 67, 69, 96, 101, 108, 130
Zervakis, Emanuel, 104, 112